RETIREMENT ISSUES, PLANS AND LIFESTYLES

PENSION PLAN VALUATION

DISCOUNT RATE DETERMINATIONS AND DIFFERENCES

RETIREMENT ISSUES, PLANS AND LIFESTYLES

Additional books in this series can be found on Nova's website under the Series tab.

Additional e-books in this series can be found on Nova's website under the e-book tab.

RETIREMENT ISSUES, PLANS AND LIFESTYLES

PENSION PLAN VALUATION

DISCOUNT RATE DETERMINATIONS AND DIFFERENCES

PATRICIA EDWARDS
EDITOR

nova publishers
New York

Library of Congress Cataloging-in-Publication Data

ISBN: 978-1-63483-238-0

Published by Nova Science Publishers, Inc. † New York

CONTENTS

PREFACE

A pension is a voluntary benefit offered by employers to assist employees in providing for their financial security in retirement. Public and private sector defined benefit pension plans are subject to different rules and guidance regarding discount rates—interest rates used to determine the current value of estimated future benefit payments. This book addresses the significance of differences in approaches used to determine discount rates among public and private plans; purposes for measuring the value of a plan's future benefits and key considerations for determining discount rate policy; and approaches selected countries have taken to choose discount rates.

In: Pension Plan Valuation
Editor: Patricia Edwards
ISBN: 978-1-63483-238-0

Chapter 1

PENSION PLAN VALUATION: VIEWS ON USING MULTIPLE MEASURES TO OFFER A MORE COMPLETE FINANCIAL PICTURE*

United States Government Accountability Office

WHY GAO DID THIS STUDY

Defined benefit plans use interest rates to "discount," or determine the current value, of estimated future benefits. Experts in the United States have disagreed on both the approach that should be taken by plans to determine a discount rate and the appropriate rate to be used. Different discount rates can create large differences in the valuation of a plan's obligations, which in turn can lead various stakeholders to draw different conclusions about a plan's health, the value of a plan's benefits, and the contributions required to fund them.

As requested, GAO examined different approaches used to determine the discount rate. This report addresses (1) the significance of differences in approaches used to determine discount rates among public and private plans; (2) purposes for measuring the value of a plan's future benefits and key

---

* This is an edited, reformatted and augmented version of the United States Government Accountability Office publication, GAO-14-264, dated September 2014.

considerations for determining discount rate policy; and (3) approaches selected countries have taken to choose discount rates.

For this review, GAO analyzed provisions in relevant federal laws and regulations, as well as financial reporting and actuarial standards. GAO also reviewed relevant literature and interviewed experts, including experts in Canada, the Netherlands, and the United Kingdom—countries with significant defined benefit systems. In addition, GAO modeled hypothetical pension investment portfolios and cash flows to calculate average investment returns using available historical data.

WHAT GAO RECOMMENDS

GAO is not making any recommendations in this report.

WHAT GAO FOUND

Public and private sector defined benefit pension plans are subject to different rules and guidance regarding discount rates—interest rates used to determine the current value of estimated future benefit payments. These differences can result in significant implications:

- Sponsors of public sector plans generally use discount rates using a long- term assumed average rate of return on plan assets. This approach results in reported obligations that generally appear lower than those of comparable private sector single-employer plans. Some experts believe this approach may encourage public plans to invest in riskier assets, which can increase the assumed return and thereby lower estimated obligations and plan contributions. Other experts believe this approach helps to maintain more predictable and lower costs. Private sector multiemployer plans generally use an assumed rate of return for funding purposes.
- Sponsors of private sector single-employer pension plans use bond-based discount rates, which are generally lower than assumed rates of return, for financial reporting of their plans' liabilities. Experts believe this approach may encourage plans to invest in less risky assets, particularly high-quality bonds, to make pension costs less volatile,

but it may increase current reported costs. Funding requirements for these plans are tied to historical interest rates, which can reduce funding compared to measures based on more recent interest rates.

Experts identified at least five purposes for measuring the value of future benefits where discount rates are used, including determining sponsor contributions, reporting plan liabilities to stakeholders, determining the amount needed to secure benefits, measuring the value of employee benefits, and determining lump sum settlement amounts. They also identified a variety of considerations in setting discount rate policy, including cost, risk, fairness, sustainability, transparency, and comparability. To address trade-offs among these varied and sometimes competing purposes and considerations, many experts saw value in reporting multiple measures of plan obligations, using different discount rates. Some experts also regarded assumed returns used by U.S. public plans as too high under current market conditions.

Selected countries we examined reported that they apply a variety of approaches to discounting. Canada requires determination of multiple measures of plan obligations, based on both assumed returns and high-quality bond rates and annuity prices. The Netherlands requires that plan obligations be measured based on market interest rates, but allows the use of assumed returns for determining plan contributions or developing recovery plans. In the United Kingdom, discount rates are determined on a plan-specific basis and can include some allowance for assumed returns in excess of high-quality bond rates, depending on plan characteristics and the strength of the sponsor. To the extent that plans in these countries use long-term assumed rates of return, they are generally lower than the 7.5 to 8 percent used by many U.S. public plans under recent market conditions. Experts GAO interviewed in these countries described a greater degree of government oversight which might help explain their use of lower assumed returns.

ABBREVIATIONS

DB	defined benefit
DC	defined contribution
DNB	De Nederlandsche Bank
ERISA	Employee Retirement Income Security Act
FASB	Financial Accounting Standards Board
FRC	Financial Reporting Council

GASB	Governmental Accounting Standards Board
IASB	International Accounting Standards Board
MAP-21	Moving Ahead for Progress in the 21st Century Act
OSFI	Office of the Superintendent of Financial Institutions
PBGC	Pension Benefit Guaranty Corporation
PPF	Pension Protection Fund
SEC	Securities and Exchange Commission
Treasury	Department of the Treasury
U.K.	United Kingdom

* * *

September 30, 2014

The Honorable Tom Harkin
Chairman
Committee on Health, Education, Labor, and Pensions
United States Senate

Dear Mr. Chairman:

Traditional defined benefit (DB) plans remain an essential source of retirement income, with tens of millions of Americans relying on them for retirement security. As of 2011, state and local government sector DB plans covered over 28 million participants, many of whom were not eligible for Social Security, and private sector DB plans covered more than 40 million Americans.[1] However, DB plans have faced a number of challenges, including the lingering effects from the 2008 stock market downturn; the implications of lower interest rates for the cost of financing retirement benefits; increased longevity of plan participants; and the possibility of a need for higher contributions to these plans. For some public plans, these challenges have been compounded by some plan sponsors not making recommended plan contributions or granting benefit increases during more favorable economic environments in the past.[2] For private plans, these challenges have occurred in the context of a long decline in the portion of private sector workers covered by such plans. While many plans have weathered these challenges, they have raised questions about the ability of some DB plans to provide adequate benefits to current workers and retirees in the future.

At the same time, experts sharply disagree on which approach should be taken to calculate these plans' estimated obligations for benefits promised to workers and retirees, referred to in this report as liabilities regardless of the purpose of the measurement (e.g., funding, financial reporting, or Employee Retirement Income Security Act (ERISA) reporting).[3] More specifically, a major source of disagreement relates to how projected future benefit payments should be discounted—or valued—in today's dollars. Discounting is based on the concept that $1 payable in the future (e.g., in 1 year) is worth less than $1 payable today because the dollar payable today can be invested and grow with interest over that year. One approach to discounting future benefits—the "assumed-return approach"—uses a discount rate based on a long-term assumed average rate of return on the pension plan's assets, typically a mix that includes substantial portions of stocks and bonds. A second approach—the "bond- based approach"—uses a discount rate based on market prices for bonds, annuities, or other alternatives that are deemed to have certain characteristics that are similar to pension promises. In many instances, a bond-based approach produces a lower discount rate, and therefore higher estimates of pension liabilities, than the assumed-return approach, particularly given recent bond market conditions and current U.S. practice in setting assumed-return discount rates.[4]

The discounting approach used can have a significant effect on the calculated pension obligations. For example, for a typical pension plan, the liability calculated using a 4 percent discount rate (a rate close to what would be produced in recent years under certain bond-based approaches, with little or no averaging or "smoothing") could be more than 80 percent higher than the liability calculated using an 8 percent discount rate (a rate commonly used under the assumed-return approach in recent years).[5,6] In addition, the appropriate discount rate can vary depending on the purpose of the measurement (see later discussion). These differences in approach to the valuations of a plan's liabilities can lead stakeholders and sponsors to draw very different conclusions about an individual plan's financial health, the value of the plan's promised benefits, the contributions required to fund those benefits, the appropriate investment strategy, and perceptions about the health of the defined benefit "system" as a whole.

As requested, GAO examined the differences of opinion concerning discount rates for pension plan valuations and funding. This report addresses the following three questions:

1. What is the significance of the differences in discounting approaches used by public versus private pension plans?
2. What are the purposes for measuring the value of a plan's future benefits and key considerations for determining plan discount rate policy?
3. What approaches have select countries taken to choose discount rates?

To address our objectives, we interviewed experts, including actuaries, economists, and other pension experts, who represent diverse points of view and a variety of organizations and constituencies. We also reviewed relevant literature on pension discount rates. In addition, we also reviewed relevant provisions in the Internal Revenue Code, the Employee Retirement Income Security Act (ERISA) as amended, relevant federal regulations, and relevant accounting standards, specifically the Governmental Accounting Standards issued by the Governmental Accounting Standards Board (GASB), the Financial Accounting Standards issued by the Financial Accounting Standards Board (FASB), the International Financial Reporting Standards issued by the International Accounting Standards Board (IASB), and relevant actuarial standards of practices issued by the Actuarial Standards Board. We also modeled different hypothetical pension investment portfolios and cash flows and calculated average investment returns using available historical data. Lastly, we reviewed approaches used in other countries by selecting three countries with relatively substantial DB coverage and ongoing discount rate discussions—Canada, the Netherlands, and the United Kingdom (U.K.)—and spoke to experts from these countries.[7] We did not conduct an independent legal analysis to verify the information these international experts provided about the laws, regulations, or policies of the foreign countries selected for this study. Instead, we relied on appropriate secondary sources, interviews with relevant experts, and other sources to support our work.

We conducted this performance audit from December 2012 to September 2014 in accordance with generally accepted government auditing standards. Those standards require that we plan and perform the audit to obtain sufficient, appropriate evidence to provide a reasonable basis for our findings and conclusions based on our audit objectives. We believe that the evidence obtained provides a reasonable basis for our findings and conclusions based on our audit objectives.

BACKGROUND

The U.S. Retirement System and Defined Benefit Plans

Employers sponsor two broad categories of pension plans: (1) defined benefit plans (DB)—in which employers generally maintain a fund to provide a specified level of monthly retirement income based on a formula specified in the plan—or (2) defined contribution plans (DC)—in which retirement income is based on employer and employee contributions and the performance of investments in individual employee accounts.[8]

Historically, DB benefits have typically been paid as a lifetime annuity (although lump sum options have increased in prevalence). Properly- funded DB plans can shield participants from numerous risks that participants face in DC plans, including eligible employees not enrolling in the plan; employees enrolling but contributing amounts likely to be insufficient, together with other sources of retirement income, to provide adequate overall retirement income; "leakage" of plan assets through withdrawals for purposes other than retirement; investment risks; and the "longevity risk" of outliving one's savings. Participants in DC plans must save a sufficient amount through contributions and investment returns to meet future retirement needs, and must adequately manage both the "accumulation phase" of building up assets prior to retirement and the "decumulation phase" of spending down assets during retirement. On the other hand, while DB plans can shield participants from numerous risks, they can sometimes be less advantageous than DC plans for workers who change employers one or more times before retirement.[9]

There are several major DB-plan sectors in the United States: (1) "public plans," which cover state and local government employees; (2) private sector single-employer plans; (3) private sector multiemployer plans, which generally cover union employees who work for participating employers in a particular trade or industry; and (4) nonqualified plans, which do not meet the applicable requirements for tax-qualification under the Internal Revenue Code and are typically maintained by employers primarily for the purpose of providing deferred compensation for select groups of management or highly-compensated employees.[10,11] We will not discuss nonqualified plans in this report because sponsors of such plans typically do not have to satisfy laws and regulations requiring a minimum level of benefits or contributions.[12]

For most private sector single-employer and multiemployer pension plans, the Pension Benefit Guaranty Corporation (PBGC) insures plan benefits, up to certain statutory limits, under separate insurance programs for these two types of plans.[13] PBGC was established under ERISA to insure the pension benefits of participants in qualified DB plans and pay participants up to the statutory limits, should their plans be terminated with insufficient funds or become insolvent.[14] The statutory limits on insured benefits are much lower for multiemployer plans than for single- employer plans.[15] In recent years, PBGC has faced large net accumulated deficits coupled with future risks posed by plan sponsors and their plans that have threatened its solvency.[16] PBGC recently reported that while its single-employer program is likely to remain in net deficit over the next 10 years, some improvement is projected. However, there is significant variation in projected results under PBGC's single-employer Pension Insurance Modeling System, with a worsening of the financial position of the single-employer program also possible.[17] In contrast, the financial status of some multiemployer plans is deteriorating. PBGC reports that the insurance fund for its multiemployer program is more likely than not to be exhausted within the next 8 years, and 90 percent likely to be exhausted by 2025, which would result in benefits for participants in insolvent plans being cut to a small fraction of current guarantees.[18, 19] PBGC uses a discount rate assumption, discussed later, to determine the present value of projected future pension benefits to be paid to the participants of single-employer plans it has taken over, and the present value of projected financial assistance payments to multiemployer plans.

In the public sector, DB plans still provide primary pension benefits for most state and local government workers. In contrast, DB plan coverage in the private sector has declined as these employers continued to shift away from sponsoring DB plans toward sponsoring DC plans. About 78 percent of state and local government employees participated in DB plans in 2013, compared with only 16 percent of private sector employees.[20] A few states offer DC or other types of plans as the primary retirement plan.[21]

Unlike in the private sector, many state and local government employees are not covered by Social Security. About 6.4 million, or over one-fourth, of state and local government employees are not eligible to receive Social Security benefits based on their government earnings and do not pay Social Security taxes on these earnings.[22] As a result, employer-provided pension benefits for such noncovered employees are generally higher than for employees covered by Social Security, and employee and employer contributions are generally higher as well. Also, unlike private sector employees with DB plans, state and local government employees generally contribute to their DB plans.

ERISA established minimum standards for pension plans in the private sector and, through the Internal Revenue Code, provides extensive rules on the federal tax effects of transactions associated with employee benefit plans. ERISA protects the interests of employee benefit plan participants and their beneficiaries by requiring the disclosure of financial and other information concerning the plan, establishing standards of conduct for plan fiduciaries, and providing for appropriate remedies and access to the federal courts, among other things. Since its enactment in 1974, ERISA has been amended many times, including by the Pension Protection Act of 2006 (PPA), which changed minimum funding standards for private sector single-employer defined benefit pension plans by, among other things, changing the measurement of a plan's funding target (including the discount rate used) and shortening the period of time over which the funding target should be attained. Minimum funding standard provisions have since been further revised by subsequent legislation. PPA also included provisions requiring private sector multiemployer plans in poor financial shape to take action to improve their financial condition over the long term.[23]

The federal government has not imposed the same funding and reporting requirements on state and local government pension plans as it has on private sector pension plans.[24] State and local government plans are specifically exempted from ERISA funding requirements, in part, because of the presumption that state and local governments can rely on their taxing power to pay for DB plan benefits.[25] These plans are also not insured by the PBGC as private DB plans are. However, in order for participants to receive preferential tax treatment (that is, for contributions and investment earnings to be tax-deferred), state and local government pension plans must comply with certain requirements of the Internal Revenue Code.[26]

State and local governments also follow different standards than the private sector for financial reporting.[27] The accounting standards for financial reporting by public and private sector pension plan sponsors are promulgated by two independent organizations. For the public sector, the GASB has been designated by the American Institute of Certified Public Accountants as the accounting standard-setter to establish generally accepted accounting principles for U.S. state and local governmental entities. GASB's standards are not federal laws or regulations and GASB does not have enforcement authority. However, compliance with its standards is required through laws of some individual states and is integrated into the audit process, whereby auditors render opinions on the fair presentation of state and local governments' financial statements in accordance with generally accepted accounting principles. For the private sector, the FASB has been designated by the American Institute of Certified Public Accountants as the accounting standard-setter to establish generally accepted accounting principles for nongovernmental entities. Those standards are officially recognized as "generally accepted" for the purposes of federal securities laws by the Securities and Exchange Commission (SEC), and companies registered with the SEC are required to comply with those standards in preparing financial statements filed with the SEC.

In addition to the standards above, actuarial standards of practice are promulgated by the Actuarial Standards Board, whose mission is to identify what an actuary should consider, document, and disclose when performing an actuarial assignment. Actuaries work with plans to develop economic and demographic assumptions.[28]

The Discount Rate and Liability Calculations

For DB pension plans, the discount rate is used in converting projected future benefits into their "present value" and is an integral part of estimating a plan's liabilities. A pension liability generally includes two pieces: (1) the present value of all projected future benefits for current retirees, as well as for former employees not yet retired but who have a vested right to a future pension, plus (2) the present value of a portion of the projected future benefits for current employees, based on their service to date (with each additional year of service adding to the liability, such that approximately the full cost of benefits is accrued when employees reach retirement).[29] The increase in the liability that arises from an additional year of employee service is called the "normal cost," which can also be thought of as the pension cost attributable to employees' work in a single year.[30] Both the liability and the normal cost depend on the discount rate, as they both represent the present value of some portion of future benefits. The higher the discount rate, the lower the plan's estimate of its liability and normal cost (see figure 1). In addition, the further into the future that the projected benefit payments occur, the more pronounced is the effect of the discount rate, because it is applied over a greater number of years. As a result, a pension liability for current workers is typically more sensitive to changes in the discount rate than is a pension liability for retirees.

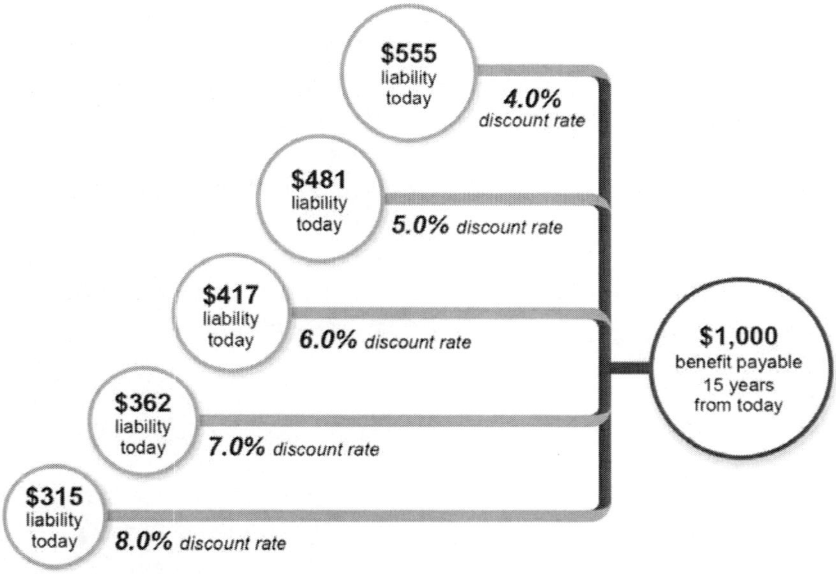

Source: GAO | GAO-14-264

Notes: The figure above illustrates the effect of different discount rates on measuring the liability for a future payment independent of an actuarial cost method.

Corresponding liabilities for a $1,000 benefit payable 7 years from today are $760 at a 4 percent discount rate and $583 at an 8 percent discount rate. For a benefit payable 7 years from today, the liability measured at 4 percent is therefore 30 percent higher than the liability measured at 8 percent. In contrast, for the benefit payable 15 years from today, the liability measured at a 4 percent discount rate is 76 percent higher than the liability measured at an 8 percent discount rate.

Figure 1. Effect of Different Discount Rates on Measuring the Liability for a Future Payment.

Approaches to Determining the Discount Rate

Methods for determining a plan's discount rate can be categorized into two primary approaches—the assumed-return and bond-based approaches.[31] The first approach—the "assumed-return approach"— bases the discount rate on a long-term assumed average rate of return on the pension plan's assets (which includes expected long-term stock market returns to the extent plan assets are so invested, and which, in recent years, and as employed by U.S. public plan sponsors, often would produce discount rates between 7 and 8 percent).[32,33,34] Under this approach, the discount rate depends on the allocation of plan assets. For example, a reallocation of plan assets into fewer bonds and more stocks can increase the discount rate and reduce the measurement of plan liabilities. Under this approach, the discount rate also depends on estimates of what future investment returns the plan will earn on its assets; more optimistic estimates produce higher discount rates and lower plan liabilities. The assumed-return approach is based in part on the premise that pension plans are long-term enterprises that can weather fluctuations in financial markets, and that the estimated long-term average cost of financing plan benefits, based on the plan's asset allocation, provides the most relevant measure of plan costs.[35]

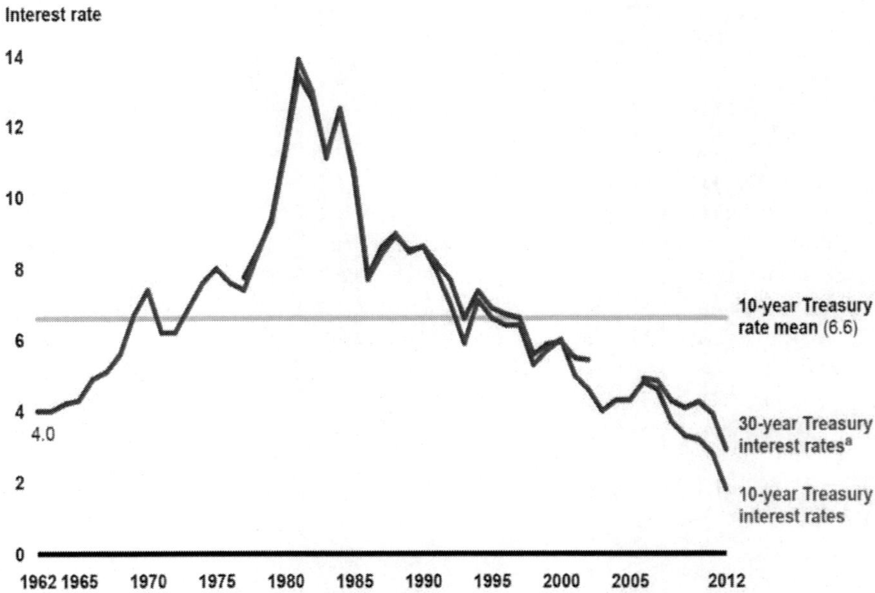

Source: GAO analysis of U.S. Federal Reserve historical interest rate data. | GAO-14-264

Note: The yields represent average rates from business days for the year.

[a] 30-year Treasury interest rates were not available before 1977 and from 2002 to 2006.

Figure 2. 10-Year and 30-Year Treasury Interest Rates from 1962 to 2012.

The second approach—the "bond-based approach"—uses a discount rate based on market prices for bonds, annuities, or other alternatives that are deemed to have certain characteristics similar to pension promises, instead of estimates of future returns.[36] The bond-based approach is premised on the theory that pension benefits are "bond-like," in that they constitute promises to make specific payments in the future, and should be similarly valued. Under this approach, the discount rate is independent of the allocation of plan assets. The relevant bond "quality" (e.g., AAA- rated, AA-rated, etc.) can depend on the specific purpose of the liability measurement, which can result in rates that vary considerably. There are at least five variations of bond-based approaches that are in use or have been proposed.[37]

- **Interest Rates on High-Quality Corporate Bonds:** This method is typically used by private sector single-employer plan sponsors for financial reporting under FASB standards.[38]
- **Historical Averages of High-Quality Corporate Bond Interest Rates:** This "smoothing" approach is allowed for funding purposes for private sector single-employer plan sponsors under amendments to ERISA and PPA, which allowed discount rates based on a 2-year average of high-quality corporate bond rates. This 2-year smoothing was lengthened to 25-year smoothing by the Moving Ahead for Progress in the 21st Century Act (MAP-21), tying discount rates to a 25-year historical average (see table 1 in the next section). The use of a 25-year historical average results in current discount rates that are significantly in excess of current or recent interest rates on high quality bonds.[39]
- **Risk-Free Interest Rates:** Another variation is to use risk-free interest rates (e.g., Treasury rates). A panel commissioned by the Society of Actuaries recommended that public plans disclose an additional liability measurement using this method, and at least one public plan currently discloses such a supplemental measure.[40] A liability based on risk-free interest rates can be thought of as approximating the amount of money that would be needed to come close to protecting the payment of future benefits from investment risk. Demographic risk would still remain, such as the risk of life expectancy improving faster than expected.[41]
- **Matching Bond Credit Quality with Estimated Riskiness of the Pension Promise:** Under this variation, as advocated by some financial economists for certain purposes, as discussed later, the bond

credit quality could be chosen to match the estimated riskiness of the pension promise.[42]

- **Annuity Settlement Rates:** This fifth variation is the method used by PBGC for its financial reporting of its deficit.[43] This method can also be considered a bond-based approach as it is based on estimated market prices for annuities, which are influenced by, and will vary with, market interest rates.[44] A liability based on an annuity settlement rate is the estimated market value of the amount of money that is required to fully insure the payment of future benefits against both economic and demographic risks.[45] As a result, a settlement liability can be significantly greater than a liability calculated using high-quality bond rates.[46] PBGC officials stated that this often leads to unpleasant surprises when a plan terminates, whereby a plan that was thought by plan participants to be overfunded turns out to be underfunded.[47] The remainder of this report focuses mainly on the discount rates used by plan sponsors and trustees.

Because bond interest rates are currently at historic lows (see figure 2), and because plans' assumed returns have not declined commensurately, bond-based approaches today that use little or no smoothing are likely to produce discount rates that are much lower than current assumed returns.[48, 49]

Defined Benefit Systems in Selected Other Countries

The discount rate approaches and regulatory structure governing pension plans in Canada, the Netherlands, and the United Kingdom differ in various ways from those in the United States. As in the United States, most Canadian defined benefit plans—both public and private—are prefunded, according to Canadian experts with whom we spoke.[50] Additionally, they noted that most plans are regulated at the provincial level, although some plans, such as those of federally regulated employers such as banks, telecommunications companies, and inter- provincial transportation companies, are regulated by a separate federal regulator.[51] Nonetheless, the regulatory principles are generally similar across all regulators, according to experts.[52] There is no national pension insurance program in Canada.[53] In the Netherlands, De Nederlandsche Bank (DNB) regulates pension discount rates.[54] An official told us that there are no regulatory distinctions among public, private, or multiemployer defined benefit plans in the Netherlands. They also noted that pension plans in the Netherlands are separate legal entities from plan sponsors, and there is no pension insurance program in place. Benefit amounts can vary with plan investment performance and plan funded status.[55, 56] In the United Kingdom, private sector defined benefit plans are prefunded and public sector plans generally are not.[57] The Pensions Regulator is the regulating entity for private pension plans and a national pension insurance program is administered by the Pension Protection Fund.[58] Plans have trustees who are autonomous from the sponsoring employers. The trustees and employers negotiate in setting plan policies, with assumptions and approaches subject to a risk-based process of review by the Pensions Regulator. According to experts, the Pensions Regulator uses what it calls a Scheme Specific Funding framework for evaluating funding requirements.[59] Discounting practices for DB pension plans in Canada, the Netherlands, and the United Kingdom are discussed later in this report, and a summary of these countries' DB regulatory requirements and discounting approaches can be found in appendix IV.

For financial reporting purposes, private sector plan sponsors in these countries often follow the accounting standards promulgated by the IASB. Plan sponsors in the United Kingdom will often follow the local U.K. accounting standards promulgated by the Financial Reporting Council (FRC) or the IASB standards. IASB and FRC standards take an approach to the discount rate that is broadly similar to that in FASB standards.

Discount Rates for Sponsors of Public Sector Plans and Private Sector Multiemployer Plans Differ from Those of Private Sector Single-Employer Plans, Resulting in Different Incentives for Both and, for the Former, Higher Reported Funded Ratios and Lower Reported Costs

Public and private sector DB pension plans are subject to different rules and guidance regarding discount rates. For purposes of both funding and financial reporting, public plan sponsors generally use an assumed-return approach, while private sector single-employer plan sponsors use a bond-based approach for financial reporting purposes, but currently are allowed a 25-year smoothing option that is generally in use for funding purposes.[60]

Private sector multiemployer plans generally use an assumed-return approach for funding purposes, but also calculate an additional liability measure under ERISA based on an average of Treasury bond rates, while standards related to discounting for accounting purposes are typically not applicable to participating employers in these plans.[61,62] These various rules and guidance result in considerable variation in the discount rates that are currently in use. The result is discount rates that are generally highest for public plans and for funding private sector multiemployer plans, followed by discount rates for funding private sector single-employer plans (under the interest rate path of the past 25 years). The lowest discount rates among U.S. plans are for financial reporting by sponsors of private sector single-employer plans and for the additional liability calculated by multiemployer plans.

Table 1. Laws, Standards, Practices, and Discounting Premises for U.S. Defined Benefit Plan Sponsors and Participating Employers, by Plan Type

Type of plan	Funding		Financial reporting	
	Applicable funding law	Discounting premise	Applicable accounting standards	Discounting premise
Private sector single-employer[a]	ERISA	High-quality corporate bond yields, which may be averaged over 25 years[b]	FASB[c]	Current high-quality corporate bond yields
Private sector multiemployer[a]	ERISA	Assumed-returnd	FASB[c]	Typically not applicable[e]
Public sector	No federal standards; each jurisdiction makes its own, if any	Generally assumed return	GASB	Assumed-return approach to extent plan is projected to be funded; bond-based approach for shortfall[f]

Source: GAO analysis of relevant ERISA provisions, FASB standards, and GASB standards. | GAO-14-264

[a] Not shown in this table is the discount rate basis used by PBGC. PBGC uses annuity settlement rates to determine the present value of future pension benefit payments to be paid to the participants of eligible private sector single-employer plans that PBGC has trusteed, and to determine the present value of financial assistance that it projects it will have to provide to multiemployer plans. PBGC uses recent prices of group annuities determined based on a confidential survey of private life insurers to derive the interest factors, or implied discount rates. A liability based on an annuity settlement rate is the estimated market value of the amount of money that is required to assure the payment of future benefits via contracts with the insurance industry.

[b] The 25-year averaging of high-quality corporate bond rates is designed to be temporary, though legislation enacted in August 2014 extends its effect.

[c] The FASB accounting standards referenced here refer to requirements for plan sponsor, and not individual plan, financial reporting.

[d] Minimum required contributions for multiemployer plans are determined at the plan level. Contribution rates for participating employers are determined by collective bargaining, but rates will typically be negotiated that are estimated to conform with minimum funding requirements. The minimum required contribution is generally based on a funding target using an assumed return discount rate. A second measure of liability, called the "current liability" and based on a 4-year weighted average of 30-year Treasury rates, is also reported by plans on Schedule MB of Form 5500. The "current liability" can affect the minimum required contribution in certain years, and is used in determining the maximum tax-deductible contribution, but the minimum funding target remains the liability measured using an assumed return discount rate.

[e] Participating employers in private sector multiemployer plans typically do not have to calculate a liability for financial reporting purposes.

[f] Under current GASB standards, public plan sponsors use an assumed-return approach. Under a new GASB standard, with implementation required by fiscal years beginning after June 15, 2014, plan sponsors would use an assumed-return approach to the extent they project that current assets, assumed returns, and future contributions for current members will be sufficient to provide for benefits; for any projected shortfalls, public plan sponsors would use a 20-year municipal bond rate as the discount rate. GASB encourages earlier application of the new standard.

Table 1 summarizes these laws, standards, and rules for different plan types. Different laws and standards also specify different actuarial cost methods and give different names to the resulting liability measures. See appendix II for more details. In addition, both FASB and GASB have differences in their requirements applicable to financial reporting by pension plan sponsors (and participating employers in the case of multiemployer plans) and financial reporting by the pension plans themselves. Under GASB standards, the discount rate requirements are the same for both plan sponsor and plan financial reporting. Under FASB standards, plan sponsors are required to discount using "settlement rates,"---which can be based on the discount rates implicit in the current prices of annuity contracts, such as PBGC's rates, but can also be based on current high quality bond rates, which plan sponsors generally do--- while plans are required to discount using best-estimate assumed rates of return. With regard to U.S. financial reporting requirements, the focus of this report is on requirements applicable to plan sponsors and participating employers, not financial reporting by the plans themselves.

Public plans and private sector multiemployer plans generally report higher funded ratios, and their liabilities generally appear lower, than those of comparable private sector single-employer plans because these plans currently use very different discount rate approaches, leading to potentially large differences in funded ratios and reported liabilities. This difference is because public plan sponsors' and multiemployer plans' discount rates are determined largely using an assumed-return approach, which generally produces higher discount rates.[63, 64] As such, this approach generally produces lower liabilities than variations of bond- based approaches with little or no smoothing (which often produces lower discount rates), as used by private sector single-employer plan sponsors for financial reporting purposes.[65] For example, Mercer, a retirement industry consultant, estimated that at the end of 2013 an average private sector single-employer plan sponsor would have a discount rate of 4.88 percent for FASB reporting. According to the National Association of State Retirement Administrators, however, public plan sponsors assumed a return of 7.72 percent on average as of December 2013.[66,67] At this difference in discount rates, the present value of a benefit payment due in 15 years for a private sector single-employer plan sponsor for financial reporting would be almost 50 percent higher than for a comparable public sector plan sponsor.[68] Some experts (including those on the GASB) view differences between public sector and private sector single-employer discounting approaches as appropriate because they see public plans as going concerns that can best estimate their pension costs using very long-term assumed returns as their discount rate. There are other experts, however, who disagree with this viewpoint or see value in both types of measures. See the next section for a discussion of various considerations underlying different views on discount rate policy.

Bond-based discount rates can vary considerably, and may not always result in significantly lower discount rates than assumed-returns.[69] In practice, there are variations of the bond-based approach that can result in discount rates that do not, to varying degrees, reflect current or recent market rates. These approaches have been implemented or proposed in order to provide stability for funding or financial reporting purposes but can have the effect of obscuring any measure of a market value of the liability (i.e., a connection to current market prices).[70] For funding purposes under ERISA as amended by the PPA, but prior to the MAP-21 amendments, private sector single-employer plan sponsors who elected to use 2-year smoothing of interest rates based on high-quality corporate bonds would have used, in December 2013, Treasury-prescribed discount rates of 1.28 percent for benefit payments due in less than 5 years, 4.05 percent for payments due between 5 and 20 years, and 5.07 percent for payments due in 20 years or more.[71] This simplified three-segment yield curve was adjusted up by MAP-21, with its boundaries tied to 25-year smoothing, to minimum rates of 4.94 percent, 6.15 percent, and 6.76 percent respectively, for the same month (see app. II for more details). In contrast, PBGC interest rate factors at December 30, 2013 were 3.00 percent for benefit payments within the first 20 years and 3.31 percent for payments beyond 20 years.[72] At these discount rates, the present value of a benefit payment due in 15 years for a private sector single-employer plan under ERISA (MAP-21) segment rates would be closer to the value determined under the average 7.72 percent assumed return used by public plans than to the annuity settlement rate used by PBGC.

Table 2 summarizes the preceding findings with regard to public and private sector discount rates.

In addition to the discount rate, the actuarial cost method used to allocate retirement costs among employees' work years can affect the size of a pension plan's liability.[73] Public sector plan sponsors typically use actuarial cost methods that assign higher liabilities to younger workers as compared to the cost methods private sector single-employer plan sponsors use. As discussed in appendix II, the cost methods typically used by public plan sponsors tend to somewhat increase the liability relative to the cost methods used by private sector single-employer plan sponsors. However, this effect is often greatly offset by the effect of the differences in discount rates determined between the bond-based and assumed-return approaches.[74]

Table 2. Some Available Discount Rate Information for U.S. Defined Benefit Pension Plans as of December 2013

Applicability	Discounting premise	Discount rate (as of December 2013)[a]
Public sector plan sponsors	Assumed return	7.72 percent average rate[b]
Private sector multiemployer plans	Assumed return	7.52 percent average rate (for the 2010 plan year)[c]
Private sector single-employer plan sponsors: minimum funding under ERISA/PPA, as modified by MAP-21	High-quality corporate bond yields averaged over 25 years[d]	Varies by timing of future benefits: 4.94 percent for less than 5 years; 6.15 percent between 5 and 20 years; 6.76 percent beyond 20 years
Private sector single-employer plan sponsors: minimum funding under ERISA/PPA, prior to MAP-21 modifications	High-quality corporate bond yields averaged over 2 years	Varies by timing of future benefits: 1.28 percent for less than 5 years; 4.05 percent between 5 and 20 years; 5.07 percent beyond 20 years
Private sector single-employer plan sponsors: financial reporting under FASB	High-quality corporate bond yields, on the measurement date	4.88 percent average rate
PBGC	Group annuity prices charged by life insurance companies, surveyed quarterly	Varies by timing of future benefits: 3.00 percent within 20 years; 3.31 percent beyond 20 years

Source: GAO analysis of relevant ERISA provisions, FASB standards, GASB standards and NASRA, Treasury, Mercer, and PBGC published rates | GAO-14-264

[a] See text for sources.

[b] National Association of State Retirement Administrators, NASRA Issue Brief: Public Pension Plan Investment Return Assumptions (December 2013).

[c] Historically, private sector multiemployer plans have often used assumed return assumptions of 7.5 percent or higher. Between 1995 and 2007, large multiemployer plans used an average assumed return, weighted by plan liabilities, of 7.57 percent. For the 2010 plan year, multiemployer plans used an average assumed return, weighted by plan liabilities, of 7.52 percent. See Department of Labor, Department of the Treasury, and Pension Benefit Guaranty Corporation, Multiemployer Pension Plans: Report to Congress Required by the Pension Protection Act of 2006 (Washington, D.C.: Jan. 22 2013). As noted earlier, multiemployer plans also calculate a "current liability" based on a discount rate that must be between 90 percent and 105 percent of a 4-year weighted average of 30-year Treasury rates. For December 2013, this permissible range, as published by Treasury, was from 3.11 percent to 3.63 percent.

[d] For plan sponsors who use this option. The segment rates in 2013 could not be less than 85 percent of the 25-year averages.

These different funding and financial reporting requirements for setting discount rates for different types of plans also result in differing amounts of discretion that plan sponsors can use in setting their discount rates. Of the GASB, ERISA, and FASB requirements with respect to discount rates, GASB standards and ERISA's multiemployer funding standards leave the most room for judgment, because, for example, estimated long-term average rates of return on pension plan investments in equities are judgments rather than observable data, and such estimates can vary significantly even among experts. This stands in contrast to ERISA's single-employer standards and FASB standards (for plan sponsors) which allow less discretion.[75,76]

Some experts said that the assumed-return approach could incentivize public plan sponsors to invest in riskier assets because doing so can increase the assumed-return discount rate, thereby lowering reported liabilities and reducing funding requirements.[77] In addition, some experts said that some public plan sponsors have sometimes inverted the recommended practice of first determining plan asset allocation—based on an assessment of investment goals and the amount of risk that can be taken on—and then deriving a discount rate based on an assumed long- term average return for that mix of assets. Instead, these experts said that some plan sponsors have set a target discount rate and then asked the plan's investment team to develop an asset allocation to support it. Other experts stated that this practice does not occur. In a related way, some experts said that the assumed-return approach has led some public plan sponsors to issue pension obligation bonds.[78] While issuing such bonds could help state and local governments improve plan funding, the increased capital into the pension fund is derived from the apparent arbitrage opportunity created for the plan sponsor by taking on more debt outside the plan. The use of an assumed-return discount rate allows the plan sponsor to capitalize on the difference between the assumed return on the invested assets and the interest rate on the pension obligation bonds, essentially taking credit for the assumed returns before actually achieving them. The use of pension obligation bonds effectively allows plan sponsors to invest on "margin," or borrow money to invest in risky assets. This strategy comes with increased risk and is only successful if the sponsor's pension assets actually do appreciate at a higher rate than the rate at which the plan sponsor borrowed.

Some experts told us that it is also possible that a plan's discount rate approach could influence future benefit levels. At the most basic level, the cost of benefits typically will appear lower using an assumed-return discount rate than using a bond-based discount rate, perhaps leading to compensation packages that are weighted toward more retirement benefits or to larger overall compensation packages. Further, some experts expressed concern that sponsors of plans that have earned more than the assumed return, such as in a bull market, have given this extra return to participants as a benefit increase, but that benefits would not be cut at the same rate during periods of low returns.[79] To the extent this occurs, it would mean that an assumed-return discount rate would need to be lowered, or the plan liability increased in some other manner, to reflect the fact that future bull-market gains would not be fully available to offset future bear market losses. On the other hand, many public plans have reduced some aspect of their benefit structure in recent years in response to low returns on assets.[80]

In contrast to the investment incentives that public plan sponsors (and multiemployer plans) may face, the use of a bond-based discount rate for private sector single-employer plan sponsors can create an incentive to invest in bonds to make pension contributions more predictable or financial reporting results less volatile.[81] For plans using bond-based discount rates (with little or no smoothing), liability values will fluctuate with changes in market interest rates. A bond-based investment policy can be used so that plan asset values will move in tandem with liability values as interest rates fluctuate. The greater the match between a plan's investment assets and the amount and timing of its projected benefit payments, the more stable the plan's funded status will be. However, holding bonds means forgoing potentially higher returns from equities. Thus, the more that a plan matches assets to liabilities by purchasing similar-duration low-risk bonds, the more expensive the plan may become to fund, which may provide a countervailing disincentive to invest more in bonds.[82] Additional incentive effects are discussed in the next section.

EXPERTS IDENTIFIED A VARIETY OF CONSIDERATIONS FOR SETTING DISCOUNT RATE POLICY AND MANY SAW VALUE IN PLAN SPONSORS REPORTING MULTIPLE MEASURES

For many of the experts we interviewed, the appropriate discount rate to use depends on the purpose of the measurement. Regardless of whether they believed the appropriate discount rate to use depends on the purpose of the measurement, all experts we interviewed pointed to various considerations that influenced their views on discount rate policy. Many of these experts supported reporting multiple liability measures and some said assumed-return rates may be too high.

For Many Experts, the Appropriate Discount Rate to Use Depends on the Purpose of the Measurement

The discount rate used can vary depending on the purpose of the measurement. There are at least five key purposes for which one might determine a discounted value of future benefits: (1) determining the required or recommended amount that the plan sponsor should contribute into the plan; (2) reporting plan liabilities to shareholders, taxpayers, plan participants, or other stakeholders, such as for financial reporting; (3) determining the amount needed to terminate a plan, settle a portion of plan liabilities, or to guarantee or minimize risk on pensions earned to date; (4) expressing the value of participants' benefits (for example, in putting a value on their total compensation); and (5) determining optional lump sum amounts payable to participants in lieu of an annuity.[83] Several experts with whom we spoke also indicated that their views on the appropriateness of different rates for different purposes of the measurement vary between public and private plans. The discussions with these experts were focused on setting future policy and not necessarily related to laws, standards, and practices that currently apply to plans in the United States.

Determining Sponsor Contributions into a Plan (Funding)

As a plan will ultimately pay benefits out of contributions into the plan and investment earnings on those contributions, some experts said a measure of a plan's liability based on an assumed return can be thought of as a best estimate of the assets a plan believes it needs to have on hand to fulfill its promises. Experts told us that an assumed-return approach can be useful in determining this amount, as well as for estimating a plan sponsor's most likely stream of future contributions into the plan. Some experts referred to this measurement purpose as "funding" or "budgeting," as distinct from "accounting" or "financial reporting."[84] For funding purposes, public plan sponsors typically calculate a liability using an assumed-return discount rate, but there are no federal laws that require them to do so.[85] In contrast, for funding purposes, private sector single- employer plan sponsors must follow ERISA standards for discounting to determine their minimum required contribution.[86] Under ERISA, private sector single-employer plan sponsors use a bond-based discount rate to determine a minimum required contribution, while private sector multiemployer plans generally employ an assumed-return approach to determine this required contribution.[87] Private sector single-employer plans include most private sector plans and about three-quarters of private sector plan participants.[88]

Reporting Liabilities to Stakeholders (Financial Reporting or Other Reports)

Another purpose for using a discount rate is in calculating and then reporting liabilities to shareholders, taxpayers, plan participants, regulators, or other stakeholders, such as in annual funding notices, or financial or actuarial reports.[89] For example, participants in private sector plans receive information on the health of their plan through the Annual Funding Notice, which reports plan funded status based on funding measures under ERISA. For single-employer plans, MAP-21 requires that this Annual Funding Notice report the plan's funded status both before and after MAP-21's 25-year smoothing of interest rates. The Annual Funding Notice can show a funded status that is higher than it would be on a PBGC basis under current market conditions. All publicly-traded companies follow FASB accounting standards for reporting pension liabilities to shareholders and other users, which allows investors to compare different companies' pension liabilities along with other financial data. For this purpose, most private sector sponsors of single-employer plans use bond-based discount rates based on high-quality (AA-rated) bonds.[90] In contrast, for public plans, the discount rate approach prescribed in GASB standards requires discounting that is closer to an assumed-return basis in most cases.[91] Some proponents of bond-based approaches for financial reporting suggested that the bond quality should vary with the riskiness of the benefit promise. For example, a pension benefit promise that was deemed to be at risk—perhaps because of some combination of an underfunded plan and a weak plan sponsor—might be discounted at a B-rated bond rate, to reflect the risk of non-payment of the benefit promise, whereas a strong, well funded pension promise by a financially strong sponsor might be discounted at a AAA-rated bond rate. This would result in a weaker sponsor reporting a lower liability than a strong sponsor with a comparable plan.[92]

Determining Funding Amount Needed to Terminate Plan or Guarantee or Minimize Risk on Pensions Earned to Date (Solvency)

To determine the amount needed to terminate a plan or to guarantee pensions to date—a "solvency measure"—the discount rate, such as the interest rate factors used by PBGC, would typically be based on the price an insurance company would charge to take over the obligation. In a standard ERISA plan termination, the plan would purchase annuities from an insurance company and transfer the liability to it.[93] This measure can also be used to determine how much it would cost to guarantee pensions at any given moment, even if the plan was not terminated. Solvency measures typically exceed the liability measure disclosed under financial reporting standards.[94] As a result, a plan could be insolvent if it needed to terminate, even if it appeared fully funded on a financial reporting basis (or on an ERISA basis). For an ongoing plan, a liability could also be calculated using Treasury bond rates, as a measure of the plan assets that would be needed to minimize investment risk in the ongoing plan, while retaining demographic risk, without transferring the obligations to an insurance company.[95]

Table 3. Some Key Considerations Identified by Experts for Selecting Discount Rates

Consideration	Summary
	Cost and risk considerations
Level and predictability of cost	Bond-based discount rates can lead to costs that are too high (depending on market conditions), or too volatile from year to year for sponsors to bear. On the other hand, an emphasis on ensuring predictable and level costs from year to year may mean plan sponsors are not contributing enough to adapt to changing market conditions.
Benefit security and risks to stakeholders	Basing funding on assumed returns increases the risk that insufficient assets could be on hand when needed, or that contributions will have to be increased, or promised benefits reduced, in the future.

Table 3. (Continued)

Consideration	Summary
Plan and sponsor characteristics	Key risk factors include the size of the plan relative to the size of the plan sponsor, the maturity of the plan, and the strength of the plan sponsor.
	Fairness and sustainability considerations
Intergenerational equity	Experts agreed that each generation should pay its fair share for pension costs, but disagreed about what this meant in practice. One viewpoint is that using assumed returns passes uncompensated risk to future generations. The other viewpoint is that using bond rates charges current generations an amount greater than the expected long-term cost.
System sustainability	One viewpoint is that the use of bond-based rates pushes plan sponsors to abandon sponsoring DB plans. The other viewpoint is that use of assumed returns leads to poor risk management practices (for both investment and benefit policy) and to crises of poorly-funded or failing DB plans that cause sponsors, or create pressures, to abandon these plans.
	Transparency considerations
Transparency and comparability	Providing a bond-based measure in addition to an assumed-return measure may help outside parties get a transparent, comparable view of plan liabilities, based on market measures. However, some experts argued that multiple measures might not enhance transparency because such information could be confusing or misleading about the likely cost to fund a plan.

Source: GAO analysis of expert views. | GAO-14-264.

Expressing Value of Benefits as Part of Compensation (Valuing Benefits)

A plan sponsor, or both management and labor in a collective bargaining process, that wants to assess the value of retirement benefits as part of employees' total compensation must decide how to discount future benefits to today's dollars, among other assumptions. All proponents of a bond-based approach with whom we spoke advocated that approach for this purpose, so that pension benefits would be valued in a manner consistent with similar future financial promises (i.e., based on bonds with a similar level of risk of nonpayment). In contrast, most proponents of an assumed-return approach with whom we spoke advocate that approach for this purpose so that pension benefits would be valued in a manner consistent with a plan sponsor's long-term budgeting estimates.

Determining Lump Sum Amounts in Plans That Offer a Lump Sum Option in Lieu of an Annuity

Some plans offer a lump sum as an optional form of payment at retirement or termination of employment, as an ongoing plan feature. Some sponsors of plans that did not previously provide for a lump sum option have recently amended their plans to offer one-time lump sum payout options to retirees and other former employees as a settlement of the plan's remaining pension obligation to those plan participants.[96] Converting monthly annuity or lifetime benefit streams into a lump sum amount requires a discount rate, among other assumptions. The Internal Revenue Code requires that a lump sum offer be at least as large as that determined using bond-based discount rates (in particular, prescribed high-quality corporate bond yields, along with other prescribed assumptions).[97]

Various Considerations Influenced Experts' Views on Discount Rate Policy

Regardless of whether they believed the appropriate discount rate to use depends on the purpose of the measurement, all experts we interviewed pointed to at least one among six considerations that influenced their views on discount rate policy. These considerations can present trade- offs in setting discount rate policy and can be grouped into issues related to cost and risks, fairness and sustainability, and transparency. (See table 3 for a summary of these considerations). In terms of costs and risks, some experts identify tradeoffs between two competing goals: having level and predictable costs versus being certain that plans will ultimately have sufficient funds to ensure benefit security for plan participants and minimizing risks to other stakeholders, including the entity sponsoring the plan, shareholders and PBGC in the case of a private sector plan, and taxpayers and beneficiaries of public services in the case of a public plan. Some experts also said that it could be useful to account for plan and sponsor characteristics in setting discount rates for funding purposes. Plan and sponsor characteristics could include the size of the plan relative to the size of the plan sponsor, the maturity of the plan, and the strength of the plan sponsor. In terms of issues of fairness and sustainability, experts disagreed on whether an assumed-return or bond- based approach to discounting would best ensure intergenerational equity for bearing the cost of these plans, and would best promote system sustainability. Additionally, experts who support the use of only the bond- based approach or both approaches identified transparency and comparability as important considerations for setting discount rate policy, but they disagreed as to whether these considerations suggested using an assumed-return or bond-based discount rate. Lastly, many experts cited financial economic theory as an important consideration in setting discount rate policy based on market valuation principles.[98] Other experts argued that this theory is not relevant to public plans because as "going- concerns" with very long time horizons, they do not have significant risk of plan termination; according to these experts, discounting based on long- term assumed-return expectations is a best estimate of long-term plan costs for public plans.

Cost and Risk Considerations

- *Level and predictability of costs* refers to the level of certainty a sponsor has that its pension costs will be affordable and stable from year to year.[99] Reported costs based on bond rates will typically be higher than reported costs based on assumed rates of return, but depending on asset allocation and amortization periods.[100] Experts also noted that liabilities based on point-in-time bond-market rates will fluctuate as interest rates rise and fall, causing costs to be unpredictable compared to costs based on assumed long-term returns, which tend to be more stable than bond interest rates because they are based on very long-term expectations.[101] Some of these experts suggested smoothing discount rates by averaging bond rates over a number of years in order to make costs more predictable, as used by most private single-employer plan sponsors under ERISA provisions. Other experts preferred that, if smoothing were to be done, that costs be smoothed directly rather than smoothing discount rates.[102] For funding purposes, private sector single-employer plan sponsors generally use a smoothing approach to discount rates, but for financial reporting, they do not.[103]
- *Benefit security and risks to stakeholders* are the risks that a plan will be unable to pay promised benefits to plan participants or will present serious financial challenges to other stakeholders, including the entity sponsoring the plan, shareholders and PBGC, and PBGC premium

payers in the case of a private sector plan, and taxpayers and beneficiaries of public services in the case of a public plan. In the private sector, some companies fail and sometimes entire industries decline. While participants in single-employer plans have PBGC protection, it is limited, and participants sometimes lose a portion of their benefits. Participants in multiemployer plans face greater risks: as noted earlier, their PBGC benefit limits are much lower, and PBGC projects that its multiemployer insurance program is itself likely to become insolvent within the next decade without further action. While states cannot and local governments usually do not go out of business and have the option to raise tax revenue or reduce services to pay for underfunded benefits, some local governments have entered into bankruptcy and some participants in public plans havelost some current benefits or anticipated future growth in benefits.[104] Benefit losses can be particularly challenging for those public sector participants who are not covered by Social Security. Some experts told us that using an assumed-return discount rate could obscure the risk that a plan could ultimately be unable to pay for benefits, and/or a sponsor may be unable or unwilling to make necessary additional contributions, even though the plan might appear fully funded on a given date using an assumed return discount rate. For example, a plan could be insolvent if it needed to terminate, even if it was fully funded using an assumed-return discount rate or a bond-based rate with significant smoothing, because the cost to actually buy out the pension benefits or transfer them to another party could be much higher than the liability using an assumed return.[105] Another risk to using the assumed-return approach cited by some experts is that a plan's assets could fail to grow at the assumed return, which would require higher-than-expected contributions or future reductions in benefits. The associated risks to participants would depend on how well the sponsor could use other financial resources to make up funding shortfalls and pay benefits. Due to these risks, according to some experts, using a discount rate that is lower than an assumed- return rate—whether a bond-based rate (with little or no smoothing) or something in between an assumed-return rate and a bond-based rate—can be viewed as a lower-risk approach than a pure assumed- return approach. Specifically, because the discount rates would be more conservative, sponsors would have to put more money into the plan to be fully funded, which would provide a cushion against the possibility of actual returns falling short of those assumed and being inadequate to pay for future benefits.

- *Plan and plan sponsor characteristics,* such as the size of the plan relative to the size of the plan sponsor, the maturity of the plan, and the strength of the plan sponsor may be key factors in determining an appropriate discount rate, particularly for funding purposes. Two supporters of the assumed-return approach for some purposes said that weak plan sponsors with uncertain futures might need to be more conservative in setting a discount rate because the sponsor might not be able to make up the difference (through higher future contributions) if plan investments perform poorly.[106] Based on interviews with experts, we identified the following key plan and sponsor characteristics to consider in setting the discount rate:
    1. The size of the plan relative to the size of the plan sponsor, since a small sponsor with a large plan may be less able to cope with assumed returns that fail to materialize. The size of a plan sponsor could be measured by metrics such as revenue or market capitalization for a corporation or revenue or tax base for a state or local government.
    2. The maturity of the plan, since an aging plan with few new participants will wind down over a shorter time horizon. Such a plan will have less time to recover if it does not meet investment expectations.[107]
    3. The strength of the plan sponsor, since a sponsor with strong revenue projections is better positioned to take risks with funding or investment policy or with its discount rate approach.

These characteristics can change over time. Indeed, it is not uncommon for a plan's demographics to mature over time, for a plan to grow in size relative to the size of the plan sponsor over time, or for once-healthy plan sponsors to become financially strained. Related to this is that risks to plans and plan sponsors are "correlated," meaning that a market downturn may both decrease the value of plan assets and weaken the financial health of the plan sponsor at the same time. These risks are also considerations in setting a discount rate.

Fairness and Sustainability Considerations

- *Intergenerational equity* is the issue of whether current and future generations bear fair amounts of cost and risk. In general, a principle of public finance is that each generation should pay for the services it receives, and that borrowing should be for capital projects that benefit people over a long period of time. Experts disagreed on how to best design the discount rate to achieve the goal of intergenerational equity. Some experts stated that using an assumed-return approach passes uncompensated risk to future generations. Others had an opposing view that using a bond-based approach charges current generations in excess of a best estimate of the funds that would ultimately be needed for future pension benefits, which would pass surplus assets to future generations.
- *System sustainability* refers to whether public or private sponsors will want to continue to provide DB pension plans under one or the other discount rate regime. Several experts attributed historical declines in private sector DB coverage to bond-based discount rate policies that created too much volatility in reported DB liabilities, along with increases in reported costs. These experts noted that DB plans are often replaced by DC plans that shift risks onto participants, who, in the view of two experts, are less equipped to bear them than are plan sponsors. Another expert noted an incongruity between the fact that bond-based discount rates create an incentive for DB plans to move out of the stock market and into bonds, whereas the standard recommendation for DC participants is to invest in a mix of stocks and bonds (with the particular mix varying by age). Some experts argued that DB plans, particularly public plans, can and should take on some amount of investment risk, which could reduce long-term costs. Others said that the discount rate should be an assumed return to be consistent with plan investment practices. Other experts argued the opposite, that assumed-return discount rates lead to poor risk management practices—such as taking on too much investment risk or increasing benefits when plans appear overfunded. In this view, such practices could lead to funding shortfalls and crises that undermine system sustainability. One such expert argued that DB pension plans should be operated more like insurance companies in their risk management practices.

Transparency and Comparability

- Transparency and comparability refers to providing sufficient information for users of financial data to understand a pension plan's financial position and to make comparisons across plans. A number of experts emphasized transparency or comparability considerations in setting the discount rate and many supported the reporting of multiple measures of liability using different discount rates. While some proponents of an assumed-return approach stated that multiple measures of liability would be confusing for stakeholders in the public plan environment, other experts were often concerned that one measure of liability reported at a single discount rate could not provide enough information for pension plan stakeholders to make informed decisions. For example, one expert compared using a single discount rate to driving across the country with only a single gauge—fuel, speed, or temperature.

Many Experts Supported Reporting Multiple Liability Measures; Some Said Assumed-Return Rates May Be Too High

Nearly half of the experts we interviewed supported the use of multiple measures for valuing pension plan obligations. Some experts saw value in reporting a bond-based liability in addition to an assumed-return liability because of various concerns about asset allocation. To the extent the same actuarial cost method is used, the difference between the two liabilities would represent: (1) a measure of the long-term reduction in cost that a plan thinks it can achieve through investments that outperform a low-risk rate and (2) the amount of investment risk a plan takes on relative to a low-risk funding target. Additionally, many experts stated that reporting multiple measures of liabilities would be useful in providing transparency. Some experts felt that more complete information for all key stakeholders would be an improvement over currently available information, while others said that reporting liabilities based on multiple discount rates would provide fuller transparency into a plan's finances than using a single rate. Some experts also took the view that public plans providing liabilities at both a bond-based and assumed-return discount rate could provide a broader range of information to plans and employers to guide plan policies, and could potentially provide a useful check on the assumed-return measurement. At least one large public plan voluntarily provides multiple measures of liability using different discounting approaches (as well as multiple actuarial cost methods). The plan discloses a number of estimates of liability based on low-risk bond rates as well as estimates of liability using assumed returns. It also provides a narrative explaining what the different numbers represent.[108] As noted earlier, while multiemployer plans generally use an assumed- return approach for funding purposes, they also calculate an additional liability measure under ERISA based on a 4-year weighted average of Treasury bond rates. Experts had differing views on the significance of this "current liability" calculation.[109]

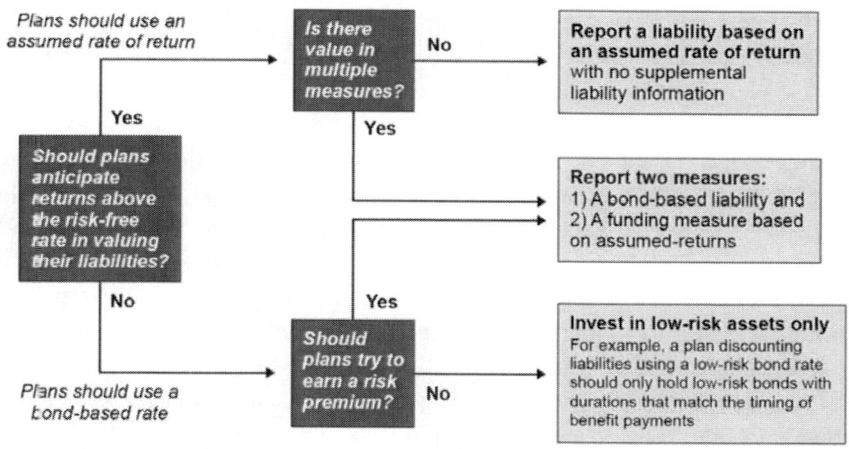

Source: GAO analysis of expert interviews | GAO-14-264

Note: The figure above illustrates how experts who principally support one approach or another can also see value in multiple liability measures.

Figure 3. Many Experts Said There Was Value to Multiple Liability Measures at Different Discount Rates.

In contrast to experts favoring multiple measures, nearly a quarter of the experts we interviewed argued that only a bond-based approach should be used to value plan obligations while nearly a third of the experts we interviewed favored use of only the assumed-return approach. For example, some advocates of each of the assumed-return and bond- based approaches did not see value in the other approach, and as noted earlier, some even saw potential damage. Some experts who saw the bond-based approach as the only correct approach for all purposes, argued that including a liability based on an assumed-return approach is incorrect based on economic theory and could result in lower contributions, higher benefits, or riskier investment strategies.

Some advocates of using only the assumed-return approach argued that including a liability based on a bond-based approach is irrelevant for public plans. One expert noted that requiring public plans to report a bond-based measure could result in pressure to fund to this much higher measure, and two experts said requiring state and local governments to fund their plans using a bond-based measure could put pressure on them to change their pension plans from DB to DC.[110] Some of these experts felt that more extensive risk analysis and disclosure, using techniques such as stochastic modeling and stress testing, would provide more useful and relevant information than the addition of a bond-base liability measure.[111]

Nevertheless, some of the experts who principally advocate for one particular approach also said that they could see value in multiple measures. Some experts who principally support a bond-based approach thought that if a plan were trying to earn returns in excess of low-risk bonds, reporting a funding target based on the assumed-return measure could be worthwhile. Some experts did not think that plans should attempt to earn a risk premium, and therefore, their assumed rate of return would be the same as the bond-based rate, since the plan would only invest in low-risk bonds. Some advocates of the assumed-return approach for at least some purposes said that reporting multiple measures could provide informational value. Figure 3 illustrates some of these lines of argument.[112]

According to some experts, even within the assumed-return discount rate framework, the returns assumed by public plans have been too high. More specifically the assumed return among most public plans surveyed in 2013 was between 7.5 to 8 percent.[113] Some experts said assumed- return discount rates are currently too optimistic, and a few said it would be difficult to achieve such returns given current market conditions. Further, some experts cited current interest rates, which are historically very low, as indicative of lower expectations for future returns. In contrast, two experts were more optimistic about future returns, including one expert who cited an analysis of price-to-earnings ratios on stocks as indicating potential for strong long-term future returns. Two experts noted that public plans' assumed returns have been declining. One of these experts said this decline indicates that the system is making necessary self-corrections. The other expert viewed the discount rate reductions as too small and too gradual.

Some experts we spoke to cited the historical returns of assets in a typical pension plan portfolio as evidence for the appropriateness of assuming a rate of return of around 8 percent. Some experts have cited, for example, the average level of historical returns over particular periods or the distribution of returns over rolling long-term historical periods, such as all possible 30-year periods for which there is good return data. However, by themselves, historical returns have limited usefulness in resolving disagreements over the appropriate discount rate. We modeled returns on typical pension portfolios over past periods, but identified numerous challenges with using historical data to generate or support an assumed-return assumption. First, analysis of returns on overlapping rolling historical periods has significant statistical limitations. Second, historical returns vary with the time period used in the analysis. Furthermore, future return expectations will depend in part on current economic variables that may not be consistent with any particular historical time period. Third, actual returns for any particular plan would also depend on plan characteristics and cash flows. Lastly, investment returns and plan benefit levels are not independent variables. Details of our analysis, and its limitations, can be found in appendix III.[114]

SELECTED COUNTRIES APPLY A VARIETY OF APPROACHES TO DISCOUNTING AND USE LOWER ASSUMED RETURNS THAN U.S. PUBLIC PLANS

Selected Countries Apply a Variety of Approaches to Discounting

Canada requires determination of multiple measures of plan obligations, based on both assumed returns and high-quality bond rates and annuity prices. The Netherlands requires that plan obligations be measured based solely on market interest rates, but allows the use of assumed returns for determining plan contributions or developing recovery plans. In the United Kingdom, discount rates are plan-specific and can include some allowance for assumed returns in excess of high-quality bond rates, depending on plan characteristics and the strength of the sponsor. Table 4 summarizes discounting practices used by plans or plan sponsors in Canada, the Netherlands, and the United Kingdom (see app. IV for more details).[115] Officials in Canada told us that Canadian private sector plans discount using both assumed-return and bond-based approaches, and then determine minimum contributions based on the greater of separate calculations using each of these two approaches to measure the unfunded liability.[116,117] In some cases, assumed returns may be reduced by a safety margin, known as a "margin for adverse deviation."[118] Canadian public plans and multiemployer plans generally are not required to use a bond-based approach for funding purposes, but they are required to calculate and provide a bond-based measure of liability to certain key stakeholders. According to a Dutch official with whom we spoke, pension plans in the Netherlands use a bond-based approach to value liabilities, with stringent solvency requirements that are adjusted for investment risk and benefit levels, so that funding targets are in excess of 100 percent of bond-based liabilities.[119,120] The official said that Dutch plans can use assumed returns for future projections of assets and liabilities, including projections to determine how underfunded plans will close funding deficits. This official also said that Dutch plans can use bond-based or assumed-return discount rates for determining minimum required contributions, but the funding target is still based on the bond- based liability. Further, when using assumed returns, the maximum expectations that can be used are regulated. In the United Kingdom, officials told us that under the Scheme Specific Funding framework that governs private plans, discount rates are plan-specific. Plans may set their discount rates by incorporating either or both of the bond-based and assumed-return approaches. Plans often use different rates to discount different portions of their liabilities by retirement status, with a more conservative (i.e., lower) discount rate at or close to government bond yields often used for benefits of retired workers as compared to some assumed return in excess of high-quality bond yields used for current workers. The precise discount rate that can be reasonably justified by a plan depends on the strength of its sponsor. The regulator uses a risk- based approach that considers plan and sponsor characteristics to determine the reasonability of the discount rate and other plan assumptions.[121, 122]

Table 4. Summary of Discounting Practices for Funding in Canada, the Netherlands, and the United Kingdom, as Described by Foreign Experts

Country	Summary
Canada	Private sector Canadian plans use two liability measurements to determine minimum required contributions: (1) a solvency-liability measurement based on bond-based discount rates, and (2) a going-concern liability measurement generally based on an assumed return. The minimum contribution requirement is based on the larger of two different "amortization" calculations, one to pay down the unfunded solvency liability, the other to pay down the unfunded going-concern liability. Most public and some multiemployer plans fund based on an assumed-return approach, but are required to provide a solvency liability using a bond-based approach to certain key stakeholders as well.

Country	Summary
The Netherlands	Plan liabilities are measured using a bond-based approach. Funding targets exceed these liabilities to provide a cushion, with the required cushion increasing with the riskiness of plan assets. Plans that are underfunded must develop a recovery plan that can be based on an assumed return. The assumed return on the equity portion of the portfolio is currently capped at 7 percent by an independent commission.
The United Kingdom	For private plans, typical discount rates currently are equivalent to using U.K. government bond rates plus about 1 percent. Under the Scheme Specific Funding framework, plans use a plan- specific approach with many plans using government or corporate bond rates for benefits of retired workers, and varying levels of assumed returns above bond rates for current workers for the period up to retirement. The discount rates used by plans depend on plan characteristics and the strength of the sponsor, subject to a risk-based review by the regulator. The regulator urges plans to consider the ability of the sponsor to assume risks of plan underfunding resulting from their discount rate and other plan assumptions. The weaker the sponsor relative to the plan, the more prudent the plan discount rate should be.

Source: GAO interviews with foreign experts. | GAO-14-264

Canada

Canadian experts said that private sector Canadian plans use two liability measurements to determine minimum required contributions: (1) a solvency-liability measurement based on an assumption of plan termination, using bond-based discount rates, and (2) a going-concern liability measurement generally based on an assumed return (and typically with projections of future salary increases).[123] The minimum contribution requirement is based on the larger of two different "amortization" calculations, one to pay down the unfunded solvency liability, the other to pay down the unfunded going-concern liability.[124] The two measurements reflect the dual goals of solvency and long-term returns. The required solvency measure reflects, in part, the absence of a pension insurance program.[125] The solvency measure generally consists of two parts: an amount for plan participants who would be assumed to take a lump sum upon plan termination, and an amount for plan participants who would be assumed to take an annuity upon plan termination.[126] Lump sum values are calculated in accordance with Canadian Institute of Actuaries standards, which specify discount rates based on a formula tied to Canadian government bond rates plus a spread.[127] For participants assumed to take an annuity, the solvency measure reflects the market prices insurers charge for immediate and deferred annuities. As noted earlier, using annuity prices can be considered a bond-based approach since such prices are influenced by, and will vary with, market interest rates. These annuity discount rates ranged from about 3.6 to 4.0 percent as of December 2013.[128]

Given the recent low interest-rate environment in Canada, private plans have generally had to fund to the more conservative solvency calculation. Experts also told us that a number of Canadian regulators have extended temporary solvency funding relief to some private sector single-employer plans following low valuations of their asset portfolios resulting from the 2008 market decline.

In contrast, experts told us that most Canadian public plans and some multiemployer plans are generally exempted from the solvency assessment for funding or have been granted temporary solvency funding relief. Experts told us that because these plans are considered going- concerns, they are allowed to make contributions based solely on an assumed-return discount rate. This is similar in concept to practices for such plans in the United States, though the actual levels of assumed- return assumptions differ between the two countries, as discussed later in this section.[129] However, Canadian Institute of Actuaries standards require that a (bond-based) solvency liability be calculated and provided by all plans, including public and multiemployer plans. An expert told us that this Canadian Institute of Actuaries requirement is not a public disclosure requirement; rather the information is provided only to plan sponsors, plan members, and regulators. Nonetheless, it stands in contrast to U.S. practice, where such a bond-based measure of liability is generally not provided by public plans.

The Netherlands

In the Netherlands, plan liabilities are measured using a bond-based approach.[130] Benefits projected to be paid within the next 20 years are discounted using a 3-month average of a market interest rate curve.[131] For benefits projected to be paid beyond 20 years, rates are extrapolated from the market interest rate curve to approach a predetermined rate, set at a fixed rate of 4.2 percent by an independent commission and introduced by De Nederlandsche Bank (DNB) in September 2012.[132] A Dutch official told us that an independent commission has recently issued an advisory on the determination of this rate. In the future, the fixed level of 4.2 percent will be replaced by a 10-year moving average of the 20- year forward rate.[133]

An official noted that the Netherlands bases a plan's funding target on the riskiness of the plan's asset allocation. Plans are subject to a base funding target of 105 percent of the plan's liability, which protects nominal accrued benefits, and a risk-adjusted target based on the riskiness of a plan's asset allocation.[134] Plans must fund to these risk-adjusted funding targets, which increase as a plan's asset allocation gets riskier in order to provide a buffer or provide a financial cushion to protect against investment risk.[135] This is in contrast to the dynamic in the United States where, under the assumed-return approach used by U.S. public plan sponsors and private sector multiemployer plans, the funding target (which is the liability) decreases as a plan's asset allocation gets riskier.

For determining minimum required contributions, plans may use either market interest rates, a 10-year moving average of market interest rates, or assumed returns. The option to use an average of market interest rates or assumed returns provides plans with some ability to avoid sharp fluctuations in minimum required contributions. However, the funding target would still be the risk-adjusted target based on the bond-based liability. For future projections of assets and liabilities, plans may use assumed returns. Similarly, plans that become underfunded must submit a recovery plan to the regulator but are allowed to use an assumed return to project their ability to close the funding deficit. However, in developing assumed returns, the maximum expectations that can be used are regulated. Currently, the maximum acceptable assumed return on the equity portion of the portfolio, as established by an independent commission as of December 2013, is 7 percent (the overall assumed return would also reflect the other asset classes in the portfolio).[136] The recovery plan details specific measures that will enable a plan to return to fully-funded status within the allotted time.[137]

The United Kingdom

U.K. experts told us that under the U.K.'s Scheme Specific Funding framework, discount rates used by private plans for funding purposes are plan-specific and may incorporate elements of either or both of the bond- based and assumed-return approaches. In setting their discount rate or rates, plans can choose to apply the bond-based, assumed-return, or a combination of approaches, which is then subject to a risk-based regulatory review by the regulator.[138] The U.K.'s Pensions Regulator urges plans to consider the ability of the sponsor to assume risks of plan underfunding resulting from their discount rate and other plan assumptions.[139] The weaker the sponsor relative to the plan, the more prudent should be the plan's strategy and approach to the discount rate (and other assumptions). A weak sponsor may find it prudent to take less risk than a strong sponsor and use a discount rate that assumes lower returns.

The Pensions Regulator told us that as part of its evaluations, the regulator places plan sponsors into one of four different categories of financial strength and conducts a preliminary screen of discount rates and other plan assumptions to determine if any appear to be too high or inappropriate given plan risks and sponsor strength.[140] The regulator cautions plan trustees in published guidance to regularly assess sponsor strength because it may fluctuate significantly over relatively short periods of time. As part of its evaluation, the regulator also compares the size of the plan relative to the size of the plan sponsor. The regulator then conducts risk-based assessments to determine which plans may require additional scrutiny.[141]

Plans are required to be fully funded or they must set up a recovery plan, which guides funding decisions until the deficit is eliminated and is overseen by the regulator. According to an official from the U.K. Pensions Regulator, plans operating under a recovery plan may assume a higher return over the recovery period than the discount rate used to calculate the plan's liability, provided that the recovery plan return assumption is justified by the investment strategy.[142] The same official also told us that about 75 percent of plans were in recovery status as of June 2013.[143]

U.K. discount rates for funding purposes frequently differ between the retired and current worker portions of the plan populations. The projected benefits of retired plan participants are frequently discounted largely with reference to U.K. government bond rates, known as "gilts," and to corporate bond rates. The projected benefits of current workers (and deferred members) are frequently discounted at gilt rates plus 2 to 3 percent for the period up to retirement. Generally, this practice acknowledges that the benefits of retirees should be discounted at a more conservative rate than the benefits of current workers, for whom more time is available to make up for any adverse plan experience, according to officials.[144] As discussed, the precise discount rate used—be it based on government bond yields or varying levels of assumed returns in excess of bond yields—is plan-specific and depends on the strength of the sponsor, subject to a risk-based review by the regulator. Currently, the net result of this plan-specific approach is discount rates of gilt rates plus 0.8

to 1.3 percent.[145] For plans in recovery, the average overall discount rate has ranged in recent years from 4.3 to 5.7 percent.[146]

As noted earlier, public plans in the United Kingdom are generally financed on a pay-as-you-go basis, with plan benefits paid out of tax revenue. Public plan sponsors make contributions to a notional pension account that are calculated based on a discounted measure of the plan's liabilities. The discount rate used for this purpose is 3 percent above the U.K. Consumer Prices Index.[147]

U.S. Public Plans Generally Use Higher Discount Rates Than Plans in Selected Countries

When determining their liabilities, U.S. public plans generally use higher discount rates than plans use in Canada, the Netherlands, and the United Kingdom. In the United States, it is common for public plans to use a 7.5 to 8 percent long-term assumed rate of return.[148] Experts told us that Canadian public plans generally use funding discount rates, using the assumed-return approach, of about 6 percent or lower, and that Canadian private plans use similar assumed-return rates for their going-concern valuations, and even lower rates—under current market conditions—for their solvency valuations.[149] According to a Dutch official, the funding discount rates used in the Netherlands, using a bond-based approach, depend on the duration of plan liabilities and can fluctuate with the market but cannot currently exceed 4.2 percent, unless amended by the Dutch independent commission.[150] In the United Kingdom, funding discount rates used by private plans in recovery have most recently been about 4.3 percent,[151] with the average excess return assumed over conventional 20 year gilts at about 1 percent.[152] In addition, discount rates for financial reporting purposes under International Accounting Standards Board (IASB) and Financial Reporting Council (FRC) standards (and FASB in the U.S.) are all bond-based and lower than U.S. public plan discount rates.[153]

Some of the differences in discount rates between the United States and these countries are accounted for by differing approaches to determining these rates.[154] Bond-based discount rates generally will be lower than assumed-return discount rates under current and most market conditions. U.S. public plans use an assumed-return approach for funding and accounting purposes.[155] In contrast, the Dutch discount rate, one of the two Canadian funding measures, and the IASB, FRC, and FASB discount rates are all bond-based.[156]

However, in those cases where these other countries use assumed returns, or some allowance for assumed returns—for example, one of the two Canadian measures, the rate for Dutch recovery plans, and the U.K.'s plan-specific approach—these assumed returns tend to be lower than assumed returns currently used by U.S. public plans.

One potential explanation for differences in the discount rates is the greater degree of government oversight in Canada, the Netherlands, and the United Kingdom, where experts said regulators routinely scrutinize discount rates.[157] Unlike for public plans in the United States, Canadian pension regulators' authority to reject an actuarial report allows them to implicitly set the boundaries for reasonable assumptions.[158] One expert stated that Canadian provincial regulators' scrutiny "sets the tone" even for plans that are not subject to solvency measurements. Another expert said that in some jurisdictions, the regulator explicitly tells plans the acceptable range of discount rates to use.[159] In addition, another expert told us that while Canadian Institute of Actuaries standards state that assumed returns should be best estimates unless otherwise required by the circumstances of the calculation, many regulators have sent notices to plans under their jurisdiction that margins for adverse deviation are needed.[160] The overall acceptable net assumption tends to vary across provincial and federal regulators but, as discussed, is generally not higher than about 6 percent, under recent and current conditions. In the Netherlands, De Nederlandsche Bank's use of prescribed bond-based discount rates obviates the need for explicit scrutiny of the discount rate assumption. However, plans are allowed to make assumed-return assumptions for recovery plans, and for this purpose an independent commission sets a ceiling on the maximum acceptable assumed return on the equity portion of plan assets. In the United Kingdom, the Pensions Regulator has legal powers to ensure that the discount rate and other plan assumptions are prudent given plan risks and sponsor strength.

Differences in discount rates also arise from variations in the regulatory framework of each country, which reflect different views among governments and regulators on the most appropriate way to protect DB pension benefits for plans under their jurisdiction. Experts told us that under the Canadian two-measurement funding standard, private plans have less incentive to be overaggressive with their assumed-return assumption used for the going-concern measurement because they must generally fund their plan using a bond-based solvency measurement, which is currently the higher of the two measures. The Netherlands' adherence to market interest valuation of accrued benefits through use of a bond-based approach to discounting for all plans is the most conservative among the countries we studied and, consequently, results in generally the lowest discount rates. As for the United Kingdom, the discretion to determine a discount rate approach under the Scheme Specific Funding framework necessitates negotiation among plan sponsors, trustees, and advisors, and may involve the regulator. This process facilitates a system of checks and balances that help to ensure that reasonable plan assumptions, including the discount rate, are used, experts said.

CONCLUDING OBSERVATIONS

Although our report illustrates the differences of opinion over pension discount rates, we found one significant area where there is some, but not universal, room for agreement. Specifically, many experts supported providing multiple measures of liabilities for different purposes to provide a more complete picture of pension plan finances. The practices of selected foreign countries—notably, Canada, the Netherlands, and the United Kingdom—may provide insight into ways that other pension systems discount liabilities, applying a variety of approaches to discounting, with significant government oversight, and generally using lower discount rates than U.S. assumed returns.

In general, as in many aspects of pension plan finances, additional transparency and information about discount rates and their impact can be useful. There may be value in providing multiple measures of liability and cost, using both assumed-return and bond-based discount rates— carefully labeled to describe their purpose (e.g., with some measures, such as funding targets, not even necessarily labeled "liabilities")—and with explanations of what these measures do and do not represent. The measurements resulting from these different discount rate approaches can ultimately improve the understanding, management, and governance of the finances of pension plans. In short, there may be value in having multiple liability measures to arrive at funding, benefit, and investment policies that will better balance risks and rewards to plan participants and all other stakeholders.

Despite the challenges that many plans currently face, traditional DB plans in the public and private sector continue to play an important role in American retirement security. This is especially true in the public sector where many current workers and retirees do not participate in Social Security and may rely on these pensions as their primary source of retirement income. Policy options to address these plans' challenges may be addressed by fostering the use of appropriate liability measurements and discount rate assumptions and increased transparency concerning their financial health. However, any such options should also be sensitive to the crucial need to ensure that benefits remain adequate to current and future retirees and their families.

AGENCY COMMENTS

We provided officials from the Department of the Treasury and the Pension Benefit Guaranty Corporation with a draft of this report. They provided technical comments that we incorporated, as appropriate. In addition, we provided officials from the Financial Accounting Standards Board and the Governmental Accounting Standards Board with a draft of this report. They provided technical comments that we incorporated, as appropriate. We also provided select experts and officials from the countries we reviewed with portions of the draft report that addressed aspects of the pension funds in their jurisdictions. We incorporated their technical comments, as appropriate, as well.

Sincerely,
Charles A. Jeszeck
Director
Education, Workforce, and Income Security

Frank Todisco
Chief Actuary
Applied Research and Methods

APPENDIX I: OBJECTIVES, SCOPE, AND METHODOLOGY

To analyze differences of opinion concerning discount rates for pension plan valuations and funding, GAO examined (1) the significance of the differences in discounting approaches used by public versus private sector pension plans; (2) the purposes for measuring the value of a plan's future benefits and key considerations for determining plan discount rate policy; (3) the approaches select countries have taken to choose discount rates. This appendix provides an account of the information and methodology we used to answer these questions.

To address our objectives, we spoke with experts, including actuaries, economists, and other pension experts, from a variety of organizations and constituencies who represent diverse points of views regarding discount rates. These experts' opinions cover a wide range of views on the appropriate way to set discount rates. We examined relevant literature on pension discount rates. We also reviewed relevant provisions in the Internal Revenue Code and the Employee Retirement Income Security Act, as amended; relevant federal regulations; relevant pension accounting standards issued by the Governmental Accounting Standards Board, Financial Accounting Standards Board, and the International Accounting Standards Board; and relevant actuarial standards of practice issued by the Actuarial Standards Board.

For our analysis of historical returns and their implications, we spoke to experts and reviewed historical data on bond and stock returns as tracked using historical data from 1926 to 2012 in the Ibbotson Stocks, Bonds, Bills, and Inflation Historical Yearbook. We calculated average annual time-weighted geometric and arithmetic returns for various asset allocations and over various time periods within the 1926 to 2012 period. We also developed two stylized pension plans—a growing plan and a maturing plan—for which we calculated dollar-weighted returns over each of the three consecutive 29-year periods from 1926 to 2012.

A growing plan is characterized by contributions into the plan exceeding benefit payments out of the plan. The ratio of cash in to cash out is set at 10 to 1 for the entire 29-year period. The ratio of contributions relative to total plan assets starts at about 40 percent in year 1 and declines to about 2 percent in year 29. A maturing plan is characterized by decreasing contributions relative to benefit payments, with benefit payments beginning to outpace contributions during the middle years of the 29-year period and continuing to increase relative to contributions for the remainder of the analysis period. The ratio of cash in to cash out starts at 3 to 1 in year 1 and ends at 0.65 in year 29. The cash in to cash out ratios for the intervening years (from 2 through 28) are determined through linear interpolation. The ratio of contributions relative to total plan assets start at about 43 percent in year 1 and declines to between 6 and 14 percent in year 29, depending on the period. These plans were provided as illustrative examples of how the dollar-weighted return of a particular plan can differ from a time-weighted return.

To examine other countries' approaches, we asked experts to identify countries with significant defined benefit systems and active controversies with regard to discount rates. Ultimately, we chose to examine Canada, the Netherlands, and the United Kingdom. These countries are not meant to be a representative sample of international practice; rather, they represent countries with contrasting approaches to discounting and ongoing discussions about the appropriate rate of discount. We spoke to experts in these countries and reviewed publicly-available documents. We did not conduct an independent legal analysis to verify the information provided about the laws, regulations, or policies of the foreign countries selected for this study. Instead, we relied on appropriate secondary sources, interviews with relevant officials, and other sources to summarize each country's approach to discounting pension liabilities. We also provided select experts and officials from the countries we reviewed with portions of the draft report that addressed aspects of the pension funds in their jurisdictions. We incorporated their technical comments, as appropriate, as well.

APPENDIX II: ADDITIONAL INFORMATION ON LAWS, STANDARDS, AND PRACTICES FOR DETERMINING DISCOUNT RATES FOR U.S. DEFINED BENEFIT PLANS

As discussed in the background, discount rate guidelines and practices for U.S. DB pension plans and plan sponsors differ for funding and financial reporting purposes, and for different plan types: public sector plans, private sector single-employer plans, and private sector multiemployer plans. As discussed, for both funding and financial reporting, sponsors of private sector single-employer plans generally use a bond-based approach, while sponsors of public plans generally use an assumed-return approach; private sector multiemployer plans generally use an assumed-return approach for funding, but also calculate an additional liability measure under ERISA based on an average of Treasury bond rates, while participating employers usually do not have to report a liability for financial reporting. However, the different plan sectors have unique guidelines and practices for arriving at a final discount rate for different purposes.[161]

It is important to note that different laws and standards specify different actuarial cost methods as well, and give different names to the resulting liability measures. For determining minimum funding requirements for single-employer plans, ERISA specifies the unit credit actuarial cost method, which defines the accrued liability based on a worker's service and salary to date; the resulting liability measure is called the funding target.[162] The Financial Accounting Standards Board (FASB) specifies the projected unit credit actuarial cost method, which is similar to the unit credit method, but adds a projection for future salary increases; the resulting liability measure is called the projected benefit obligation, also frequently referred to as the PBO.[163] The recently issued Governmental Accounting Standards Board (GASB) revisions specify that plan sponsors use the entry age actuarial cost method. Using this method, a worker's service and salary are both projected to retirement to estimate a projected benefit. The cost of this benefit is allocated over the worker's entire service (both past and projected future) as a level percentage of his or her salary (for plans whose benefit formula is tied to salary levels). The accrued liability is the value of these allocated costs accumulated up to the point of the worker's service to date. The resulting liability measure is simply called the total pension liability. For active workers, holding actuarial assumptions constant, an entry age normal accrued liability (GASB method) will typically be somewhat higher than a projected unit credit accrued liability (FASB method), which in turn will typically be somewhat higher (for benefit formulas tied to salary levels) than a unit credit accrued liability (ERISA method). For plan participants who are already retired or terminated employment, these three methods produce the same liability.

Table 5. Laws, Standards, Practices, and Discounting Premises for U.S. Defined Benefit Plan Sponsors and Participating Employers, By Plan Type

Type of plan	Funding		Financial Reporting	
	Applicable funding law	Discounting Premise	Applicable accounting standards	Discounting premise
Private sector single-employer[a]	ERISA	High-quality corporate bond yields, which may be averaged over 25 years[b]	FASB[c]	Current high-quality corporate bond yields
Private sector multiemployer[a]	ERISA	Assumed-return[d]	FASB[c]	Typically, notapplicable[e]

Table 5. (Continued)

Type of plan	Funding		Financial Reporting	
Public sector	No federal standards; each jurisdiction makes its own, if any	Generally, assumed return	GASB	Assumed-return approach to extent plan isprojected to be funded; bond-based approach for shortfall[f]

Source: GAO analysis of relevant ERISA provisions, FASB standards, and GASB standards. | GAO-14-264

[a] Not shown in this table is the discount rate basis used by PBGC. PBGC uses annuity settlement rates to determine the present value of future pension benefit payments to be paid to the participants of eligible private sector single-employer plans that PBGC has trusteed, and to determine the present value of financial assistance that it projects it will have to provide to multiemployer plans. PBGC uses recent prices of group annuities determined based on a confidential survey of private life insurers to derive the interest factors, or implied discount rates. A liability based on an annuity settlement rate is the estimated market value of the amount of money that is required to assure the payment of future benefits via contracts with the insurance industry.

[b] The 25-year averaging of high-quality corporate bond rates is designed to be temporary, though legislation enacted in August 2014 extends its effect.

[c] The FASB accounting standards referenced here refer to requirements for plan sponsor, and not individual plan, financial reporting.

[d] Minimum required contributions for multiemployer plans are determined at the plan level. Contribution rates for participating employers are determined by collective bargaining, but rates will typically be negotiated that are estimated to conform with minimum funding requirements. The minimum required contribution is generally based on a funding target using an assumed return discount rate. A second measure of liability, called the "current liability" and based on a 4-year weighted average of 30-year Treasury rates, is also reported by plans on Schedule MB of Form 5500. The "current liability" can affect the minimum required contribution in certain years, and is used in determining the maximum tax-deductible contribution, but the minimum funding target remains the liability measured using an assumed return discount rate.

[e] Participating employers in private sector multiemployer plans typically do not have to calculate a liability for financial reporting purposes.

[f] Under current GASB standards, public plan sponsors use an assumed-return approach. Under a new GASB standard, with implementation required by fiscal years beginning after June 15, 2014, plan sponsors would use an assumed-return approach to the extent they project that current assets, assumed returns, and future contributions for current members will be sufficient to provide for benefits; for any projected shortfalls, public plan sponsors would use a 20-year municipal bond rate as the discount rate. GASB encourages earlier application of the new standard.

In addition, the different funding and financial reporting requirements for setting discount rates for different types of plans also result in differing amounts of discretion that plan sponsors can use in setting their discount rates. Of the GASB, ERISA, and FASB requirements with respect to discount rates, GASB standards and ERISA's multiemployer funding standards leave the most room for judgment, because, for example, estimated long-term average rates of return on pension plan investments in equities are judgments rather than observable data, and such estimates can vary significantly even among experts. This stands in contrast to ERISA's single-employer standards and FASB standards (for plan sponsors) which allow less discretion.[164, 165] Table 5 summarizes differences in the laws, standards, and practices that govern discount rate approaches across plan types in the United States.

GASB Standards

Recently revised GASB standards prescribe a "blended approach" to determining pension discount rates for financial reporting by public plan sponsors, with implementation required by fiscal years beginning after June 15, 2014. Under the new GASB standard, plan sponsors would use an assumed-return approach to the extent they project that current assets, assumed returns, and future contributions for current members will be sufficient to provide for benefits; for any projected shortfalls, public plan sponsors would use 20-year, tax-exempt general obligation municipal bond interest rates with an average rating of AA/Aa or higher. Thus, for some plans the composite discount rate will be a hybrid of the assumed-return approach and bond-based approach. Industry experts have indicated that, on average, the composite discount rate is likely to be closer to the assumed-return rate for two reasons: many plans have contribution policies which, combined with current plan assets, are likely to be projected to cover projected benefit payments, so that the blended discount rate will be the same as the assumed-return discount rate; and for those plans where there is a projected insufficiency, the bond-based approach would only apply to a portion of plan liabilities.

ERISA Requirements

With regard to the rates they use to discount benefits, single-employer sponsors are generally required to use a bond-based approach to determine the minimum required contribution. However, within this framework, these sponsors have options which can result in measurements of plan liabilities that may not be closely tied to current market conditions. Plan sponsors are given the option of using a full yield curve approach, which matches projected benefit payments to high- quality corporate bond interest rates averaged over a current month, so that under this option, the measurement of plan liabilities would be tied to current or recent market conditions. A plan choosing this approach would discount a benefit payment due in 10 years at the yield curve rate as published by Treasury for year 10. However, single-employer plan sponsors may also elect to discount using a simplified three-segment yield curve published by Treasury, with the three different segment interest rates applicable to benefit payments due in less than 5 years, 5 to 20 years, and 20 years or more. These segment rates are based on a 2- year average of bond rates and also cannot be higher or lower than maximum and minimum segment rates as set in law in 2012 as part of the Moving Ahead for Progress in the 21st Century Act (MAP-21).[166] The MAP-21 maximum and minimum apply to plans that use the segment rate approach, and are based on long-term (25-year) bond averages. MAP-21's effect on discount rates is designed to be temporary. Because average interest rates over the past 25 years are significantly higher than more recent market rates, the MAP-21 changes had the effect of significantly increasing ERISA discount rates over what they would otherwise have been, thereby lowering measurements of plan liabilities and reducing minimum funding requirements.[167]

Under the bond-based approach used by private sector single-employer pension plans under ERISA (as well as common practice under FASB), a single pension plan will use different discount rates to calculate the present value of benefits that will be paid out at different points in the future. This means that different plans can end up with very different average rates of discount depending on the age of the plan's participants. In contrast, a public plan using an assumed rate of return would typically discount all future benefit payments at the same assumed return. Because the assumed return is based on asset allocation, the rates will vary depending on how a plan allocates its assets. This is an example of how the bond-based approach determines discount rates based on characteristics of a plan's liabilities, whereas the assumed-return approach determines discount rates based on characteristics of the assets being used to finance the liabilities. As discussed, under ERISA, private sector multiemployer plans generally discount using an assumed rate of return for funding purposes. However, these plans also calculate a liability based on a bond-based discount rate under ERISA, which can sometimes affect the timing of minimum required contributions and is also used in the calculation of the maximum deductible contribution. Experts had differing views of the significance of the reporting of this measure.

FASB Standards

FASB financial reporting standards are separate from ERISA funding standards but plan sponsors also typically use high-quality corporate bond rates to compute liabilities, with some key differences.[168] The corporate bond rates that plan sponsors use to satisfy FASB standards are snapshots of market interest rates on the measurement date, producing liabilities based on current market interest rates. This approach is different from discount rates based on ERISA segment rates, which are averages of past and present rates. Also, FASB standards allow companies to select a hypothetical matching bond portfolio, or a yield curve (extrapolated for projected benefits with long durations), rather than rely on one particular set of published rates (such as those produced by Treasury for ERISA). Also, unlike the ERISA funding target, which is based on worker's service and salary to date, FASB requires companies to report a projected benefit obligation, which for pension benefit formulas based on compensation includes an assumption of future benefit growth due to salary increases.

APPENDIX III: HISTORICAL RETURNS AND THE DISCOUNT RATE

Challenges with Analysis of Historical Returns

Even though some experts we spoke to cited the historical returns of assets in a typical pension plan portfolio as evidence for the appropriateness of assuming a rate of return of around 8 percent, we found several challenges with using historical data to generate or support an assumed-return assumption. First, reliance on returns during overlapping rolling historical periods has significant statistical limitations. Second, historical returns vary with the time period used in the analysis. Furthermore, future return expectations will depend in part on current economic variables that may not be consistent with any particular historical time period. Third, actual returns for any particular plan would also depend on plan characteristics and cash flows. Fourth, investment returns and plan benefit levels are not independent variables. Also, the potential use of historical returns is only relevant within the context of an assumed-return approach to discounting because a bond-based approach relies on observable market prices for bonds, annuities, or other alternatives.[169]

Rolling Period Historical Returns Present Statistical Challenges

Using rolling period analysis based on historical returns to support an assumed-return discount rate presents statistical challenges that limit any conclusions that can be drawn. Some experts have argued that pension plans have a long time horizon and can bear short-term investment volatility because the historical record shows lower investment risk over long time horizons, such as 30 years.[170] The historical record of reliable capital market returns covers 87 years, from 1926 through 2012.[171] These 87 years contain 58 full consecutive, rolling 30-year periods (i.e., 1926-1955, 1927-1956, etc., through 1983-2012). However, the returns over these 58 different 30-year periods are not statistically independent, since they contain overlapping years. In fact, the 87 years from 1926 to 2012 contain fewer than three independent 30-year data points.[172] Further, the 58 30-year rolling periods are heavily skewed towards the middle years of the 1926 to 2012 period.[173] As a result of these limitations, we cannot draw conclusions about investment risk over 30-year periods solely from this historical record.

Past Returns Depend on the Time Period Used in the Analysis, and Future Returns Depend on Current Economic Variables

In analyzing the 1926-2012 historical period, modeled returns vary with particular subsets of years during this historical period and with the assumed allocation of plan assets. For the entirety of this 87-year historical period, we found that a static portfolio allocation of 60 percent in equities and 40 percent in corporate bonds ("60/40 portfolio"), rebalanced annually and with no intervening net cash flows, would have achieved an 8.9 percent annualized nominal return.[174] However, when "trailing returns" (i.e., returns for the years leading up to the current year) are used to examine historical capital market performance, the historical time period chosen can greatly affect return expectations. For example, as figure 4 shows, for the same 60/40 portfolio, the annualized nominal returns are 6.5 percent over the past 15 years, 10.9 percent over the past 30 years, 9.3 percent over the past 50 years, 8.7 percent over the past 85 years, and again, 8.9 percent over the past 87 years. Even to the extent that such information can be informative as to future expectations, it is not clear how to assign relative credibility between the more recent and the more distant past.

When we analyzed returns over all 58 30-year periods within the 1926-2012 historical period, we found that annualized nominal returns for the 60/40 portfolio ranged from a low of 7.3 percent to a high of 12.5 percent. In contrast, for a 100 percent corporate bond portfolio, the annualized nominal returns ranged from a low of 1.8 percent to a high of 10.8 percent. However, because the 58 periods are not statistically independent, these ranges understate the amount of variability in returns one might expect in future 30-year periods.

In addition, experts told us that expectations about future returns also need to be informed by current economic variables. Experts mentioned in particular the current level of interest rates and the current price-to- earnings ratios on equities. Any historical period may have had very different starting levels for these two variables.

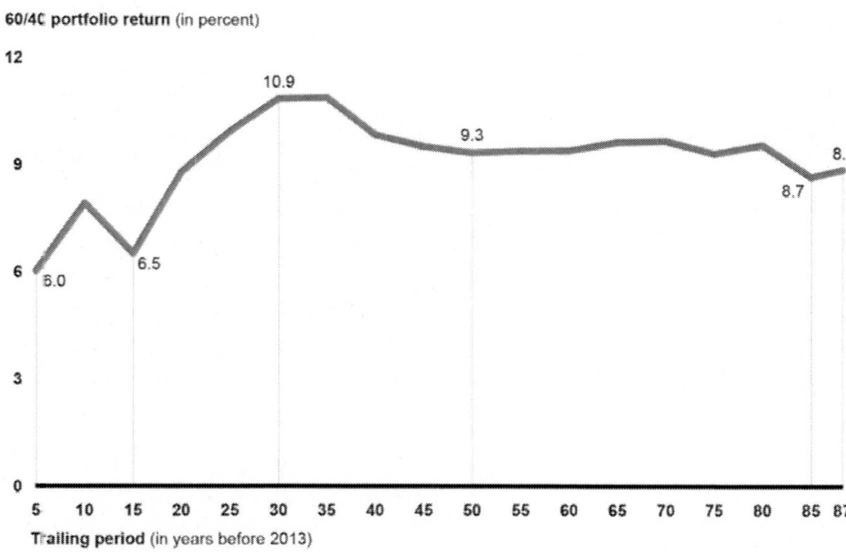

Source: GAO analysis of ibbostson historical return data. | GAO-14-264

Figure 4. Annualized Historical Returns for Different Trailing Periods.

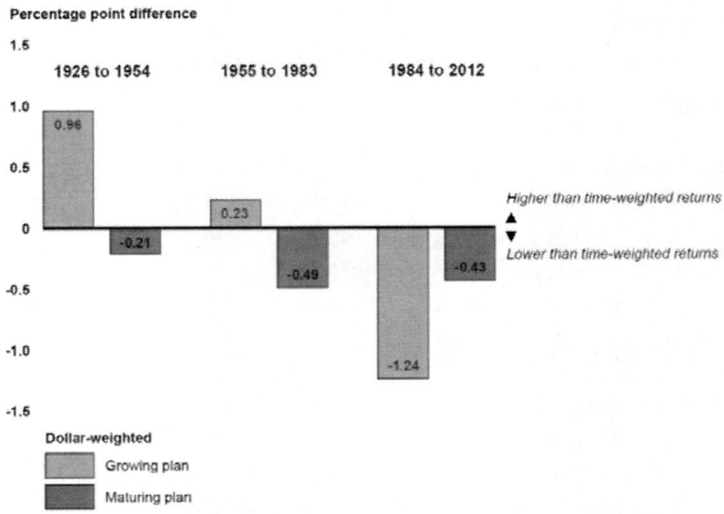

Source: GAO analysis of ibbostson historical return data. | GAO-14-264

Figure 5. Return Differential between Hypothetical Plans and Time-weighted Averages.

Returns Also Depend on Plan Characteristics and Cash Flows

Another challenge to drawing conclusions from historical returns is that any approach may not reflect the cash flow patterns of an actual pension plan. Historical return statistics are often "time-weighted" averages, meaning that they reflect average returns over some time period that are independent of the order in which those historical returns occurred. Time-weighted returns do not vary across plans. Of more relevance to an actual pension plan is its "dollar-weighted" average return, which reflects the plan's cash flow pattern. For example, consider a 10-year period in which returns average 10 percent annually for the first 5 years and 2 percent annually for the second 5 years, for a 10-year average of 6 percent annually, which is the time-weighted average return.[175] However, for a growing pension plan that has net cash inflows (contributions paid in exceeding benefits paid out) during this period, the returns in the second half of the period may be more important than the returns in the first half of the period, because there may be more money at stake in the second half of the period. Consequently, if a growing plan experiences decreasing rates of return, the plan's dollar-weighted average return may be less than the time-weighted average.

To apply this concept to our historical return analysis, we developed two hypothetical pension plans—a growing plan and a maturing plan.[176] Each of these hypothetical plans generated a unique cash flow pattern that broadly reflected its plan characteristics and certain assumptions about the plans.[177] We divided the 87-year period from 1926 to 2012 into three discrete 29-year periods.[178] For each hypothetical plan, we calculated dollar-weighted returns for each period based on plan assets invested in various investment portfolio allocations using historical return data.

Our analysis shows that for a 60/40 investment portfolio allocation to stocks and corporate bonds, the dollar-weighted returns of our hypothetical plans can differ significantly from time-weighted returns. The hypothetical growing plan outperformed the time-weighted average in two of the three 29-year historical periods, while the maturing plan underperformed the time-weighted average in all three periods. As figure 5 shows, the hypothetical growing plan would return nearly one percentage point above the time-weighted average return for the period from 1926 to 1954 and almost a quarter of a percentage point above the time-weighted return for the period from 1955 to 1983, but the maturing plan would return nearly 1.25 percent below the time-weighted average return for the period from 1984 to 2012.

Investment Returns and Benefit Levels Are Not Independent, Potentially Diminishing Effective Returns

Many experts cited examples of pension plans for which benefit formulas were increased following periods of robust investment returns. We have also seen examples in more recent years of benefit formulas being decreased in financially distressed plans.[179] These examples indicate that investment returns and benefit levels have not been independent variables. If plan benefits have been more flexible in this way on the upside than the downside—an empirical question—it would mean that some historical investment returns effectively went towards net benefit increases rather than supporting previously existing benefit promises. This is another reason for caution in looking to historical returns to support a particular discount rate.

Geometric versus Arithmetic Means

In calculating average annual historical returns, either of two types of time-weighted (i.e., plan-independent) average annual returns can be measured—geometric average return or arithmetic average return. For returns that vary from year to year, the geometric average will always be less than an arithmetic average.[180] Figure 6 shows the differences in these two types of average returns for a 60/40 investment portfolio allocated to stocks and corporate bonds calculated for various trailing periods.

As a simplified but illustrative example, consider a two-year historical period where the return is positive 100 percent in year one and negative 50 percent in year two. One dollar invested at the start of this period will grow to 2 dollars at the end of year one and then fall back to 1 dollar at the end of year two, for a total net return of zero over the 2-year period. The geometric average return is zero. The arithmetic average return is positive 25 percent (100 percent minus 50 percent, divided by 2).

Experts we spoke with disagreed about whether a forward-looking assumed-return assumption should reflect a geometric average expectation or an arithmetic average expectation. Conceptually, a geometric assumption reflects a median expectation (with a 50 percent chance that actual investment performance will be above or below the assumption) while an arithmetic assumption reflects a mean (average) expectation (with a greater than 50 percent chance that actual investment performance will fall short of the assumption).

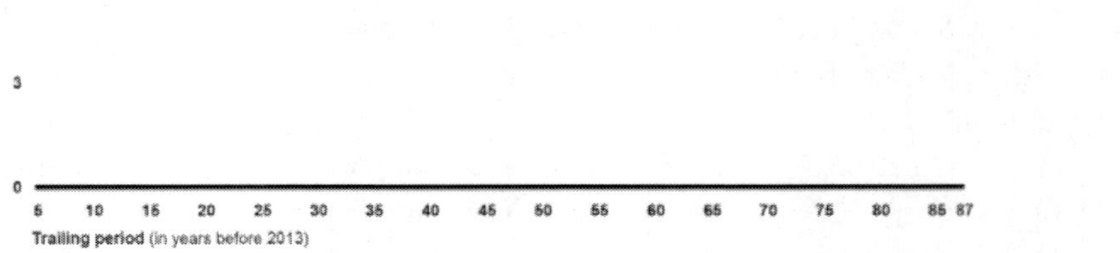

Source: GAO analysis of ibbostson historical return data. | GAO-14-264

Figure 6. Arithmetic Means Are Higher Than Geometric Means.

Appendix IV: Key Features of Discount Rate Practices in Canada, the Netherlands, and the United Kingdom

Canada

At a Glance

- As of 2011, 38 percent of Canadian employees were covered under a registered pension plan in Canada.[181] Of those, 74 percent or nearly 4.5 million Canadians were participants in defined benefit plans, with an aggregate market value of assets of about 1.1 trillion Canadian dollars.
- Defined benefit plans are generally regulated at the provincial level, with some regulated by a separate federal regulator, so policies can vary by province and the federal level. Most defined benefit plans, both public and private, are prefunded.
- With the exception of Ontario province, which has pension insurance that insures a nominal benefit of up to one thousand Canadian dollars per month, there is no pension insurance program in Canada.

Source: GAO analysis of foreign agency documents and interviews with Canadian officials and industry experts; U.S. State Department (base map); Art Explosion (flags). | GAO-14-264

Note: GAO did not conduct an independent legal analysis of the laws, regulations, or policies of the countries selected for this review.

Funding Requirements and Discounting Approaches

- There are two liability assessments that determine minimum required contributions—a solvency valuation using bond-based discount rates and a going-concern valuation generally based on an assumed-return on plan assets. The solvency measurement typically does not include a projection of future salary increases while the going-concern measurement typically does include projections of future salary increases. Assumed return assumptions sometimes are reduced by a margin for adverse deviation.[182]

- Generally, private sector plans discount using both the bond-based and the assumed-return approach, and then determine minimum contributions based on the greater of separate calculations using each of these two approaches to measure the unfunded liability. A number of Canadian regulators have extended temporary solvency funding relief to some private single-employer plans following low valuations of their asset portfolios resulting from the 2008 market decline.
- Generally, most public plans and some multiemployer plans have been exempted from the solvency assessment for funding purposes, or have been granted temporary solvency funding relief, as they are considered going-concerns. These plans make contributions based on an assumed-return discount rate. However, these plans must also provide a solvency-based liability measure to plan sponsors, plans members, and regulators.
- The bond-based rates used in the solvency assessment reflect a combination of (i) a formula tied to Canadian government bond rates plus a spread intended to approximate the results that would be obtained from discounting using a full yield curve based on highly rated provincial bonds (for participants who would be assumed to take a lump sum), and (ii) the market prices insurers charge for immediate and deferred annuities (for participants who would be assumed to take an annuity).
- Although the assumed-return rate used in the going-concern assessment is similar in concept to the approach applied by public sector plans and private sector multiemployer plans in the U.S., the return assumptions differ between the two countries, with assumed returns in Canada typically at 6 percent or lower, reflecting both lower best-estimates of assumed returns and, in some cases, the subtraction of a margin for adverse deviation.
- For financial reporting purposes, private sector plan sponsors in Canada often follow the accounting standards promulgated by the International Accounting Standards Board (IASB).

Regulator and Regulatory Principles

- At the federal level, the Office of the Superintendent of Financial Institutions (OSFI) regulates and supervises private pension plans in federally regulated areas of employment, such as banking, telecommunications and inter-provincial transportation. Each province has its own regulatory body for pension plans under its jurisdiction.[183] The majority of registered defined benefit pension plans are under the jurisdiction of either the regulator in Ontario, Quebec, or with the OSFI.

- Regulatory principles are generally similar across all regulators, whether provincial or federal.[184]
- Generally, provincially-regulated plans are assessed once every three years, while federally-regulated plans and plans registered with the Québec regulator are assessed annually.
- Canadian regulators have the authority to reject an actuarial report which allows them to implicitly set boundaries for reasonable assumptions.

Netherlands

At a Glance

- In 2013, defined benefit plans accounted for 78 percent of all retirement plans in the Netherlands. Participants in those plans represented nearly 93 percent of all active pension plan participants.
- With regard to the discount rate, the regulator makes no regulatory distinctions between public, private, or multiemployer defined benefit pension plans.
- Pension plans are separate legal entities from plan sponsors and there is no pension insurance program.
- Plan benefits can vary with investment performance and funded status.

Source: GAO analysis of foreign agency documents and interviews with Dutch officials and industry experts; U.S. State Department (base map); Art Explosion (flags). | GAO-14-264

Note: GAO did not conduct an independent legal analysis of the laws, regulations, or policies of the countries selected for this review.

Funding Requirements and Discounting Approaches

- All plans discount their liabilities using a bond-based approach.[185] Benefits projected to be paid within the next 20 years are discounted using a 3-month average of the Euro interest rate swap curve. For benefits projected to be paid beyond 20 years, rates are extrapolated from the swap curve to approach a predetermined Ultimate Forward Rate, currently set at a fixed rate of 4.2 percent by an independent commission and introduced by the De Nederlandsche Bank in September of 2012. In the future, the fixed level of 4.2 percent will be replaced by a 10-year moving average of the 20-year forward rate.[186]

- To safeguard nominal accrued benefits, plans must be funded to a base funding target of 105 percent using prescribed market interest rates. Plans can attempt to provide inflation indexed benefits by investing in riskier asset portfolios. Inflation indexed benefits are granted only to the extent they are supported by actual investment returns. However, base funding targets are also "risk-adjusted," meaning the base funding target is increased the riskier the plan's asset allocation, in order to provide a buffer against investment risk. An official told us that a common asset allocation of 50 percent equity, 40 percent bond, and 10 percent real estate would require a plan to be120 percent funded, based on a 2.5 percent probability of shortfall in a 1-year horizon.
- For determining minimum required contributions, plans may use either market interest rates, a 10-year moving average of market interest rates, or assumed returns. However, the funding target would still be the risk-adjusted target based on the bond-based liability.
- For future projections of assets and liabilities, plans may use assumed returns.
- Plans in recovery are allowed to assume investment returns based on plan asset allocation to project reaching funding targets within the recovery period.
- Plans with funded ratios less than the 105 percent base funding target must submit a recovery plan to return to full funding within 3 years.[187] Nominal accrued benefits can be reduced for plans that do not achieve the base funding target within this allotted time. Plans with funded ratios less than the risk-adjusted funding target (specific to the plan's asset al.location) must reduce or eliminate inflation-indexation and submit a recovery plan to return to this funding target within 15 years.
- For financial reporting purposes, private sector plan sponsors in the Netherlands often follow the accounting standards promulgated by the International Accounting Standards Board (IASB).

Regulator and Regulatory Principles

- De Nederlandsche Bank (DNB) examines the financial position of pension funds and regulates discount rates. The Netherlands Authority for the Financial Markets monitors market conduct relating to pension funds' obligations to provide information to members.
- The DNB publishes discount rates on a monthly basis.
- Pension plans must submit quarterly and annual reports to the DNB.
- When using assumed returns, the maximum expectations that can be used are regulated. Currently, the maximum acceptable assumed return on the equity portion of the portfolio, as established by an independent commission, is 7 percent (the overall assumed return would also reflect the other asset classes in the portfolio).[188]

The United Kingdom

At a Glance

- In 2012, participation in workplace pension plans was at 46 percent.[189] 91 percent of public sector employees with workplace pensions had a defined benefit plan while 26 percent of private sector employees with workplace pensions were in such plans. Overall, the proportion of employees with defined benefit pension plans continued to fall, with 28 percent of employees participating in such plans in 2012, compared with 46 percent in 1997.
- Private sector defined benefit plans are almost always prefunded while public sector plans are generally pay-as-you-go, with benefits paid out of tax revenue (the discussion in this report is focused primarily on U.K. private sector plans).
- Trustees of private plans are autonomous from the sponsoring employer. Trustees and employers negotiate in setting plan policies, with assumptions, including the discount rate, and methods subject to a risk-based review by the Pensions Regulator.
- A national pension insurance program administered by the Pension Protection Fund (PPF) provides compensation to members of eligible, largely private sector defined benefit pension plans when there is a qualifying insolvency event in relation to the employer, and where

there are insufficient assets in the pension plan to cover the PPF level of compensation.

Source: GAO analysis of foreign agency documents and interviews with U.K. officials and industry experts; U.S. State Department (base map); Art Explosion (flags). | GAO-14-264

Note: GAO did not conduct an independent legal analysis of the laws, regulations, or policies of the countries selected for this review.

Funding Requirements and Discounting Approaches

- There is no standard actuarial method or assumptions that defined benefit pension plans must use beyond the requirements that actuarial valuations must use an accrued benefit method, assets must be at market value, and economic and actuarial assumptions must be chosen prudently based on circumstances specific to the plan. Regulations specifically allow plans to use either a bond-based, assumed-return, or a combination of both approaches to determine its discount rate for funding purposes.[190]
- Under U.K.'s Scheme Specific Funding framework, discount rates used by private plans for funding purposes are plan-specific and may incorporate elements of both the bond-based and assumed-return approaches.
- Regulator guidance cautions sponsors to consider the strength of the employer sponsor to support the plan, known as the "employer covenant," in plan assumptions. A strong sponsor can have some justification for using a somewhat higher discount rate, but the regulator cautions plan trustees to regularly assess sponsor strength because it may be subject to significant variation over relatively short periods of time. Conversely, a weak sponsor may find it prudent to take less risk and use a discount rate that assumes lower returns above safe bond yields.
- Discount rates for funding purposes frequently differ between the retired and current worker portions of the plan populations. The projected benefits of retired plan participants are frequently discounted largely with reference to U.K. government bond rates, known as "gilts," and to corporate bond rates. The projected benefits of current workers (and deferred members) are frequently discounted at gilt rates plus 2 to 3 percent for the period up to retirement.

- Plans under recovery are allowed to assume a higher return, over the recovery period, than the discount rate used to calculate the plan's liability.
- For financial reporting purposes, private-sector plan sponsors in the United Kingdom often follow accounting standards promulgated by the local Financial Reporting Council (FRC) or the International Accounting Standards Board (IASB). [191] FRC and IASB standards take an approach to the discount rate that is broadly similar to FASB in the United States.

Regulator and Regulatory Principles

- The Pensions Regulator is responsible for regulating work-based pension plans, which includes occupational defined benefit and defined contribution plans as well as certain aspects of work-based personal pensions. It has the authority to oversee the administration of these plans and contributions made to them based on its objective to protect the benefits under occupational pension plans of, or in respect to, members of such plans.
- Private plan sponsors must prepare actuarial valuations on at least a triennial basis (provided they also produce annual updates-–otherwise they have to do annual valuations). Plans in deficit, and which have therefore prepared a recovery plan, must submit details of the recovery plan and valuation to the regulator. Plans in surplus must submit details of their valuation along with their regular plan data updates. The regulator conducts a risk-based assessment to determine if additional scrutiny or actions are necessary.

End Notes

[1] Coverage refers to all active, inactive, and retired plan participants, as well as beneficiaries. State and local government DB plan sector participation data are based on fiscal years that ended between July 1, 2010 and June 30, 2011 (fiscal year 2011), with some exceptions. Private sector DB plan sector participation data is based on Form 5500 filings for plan years ending in 2011. See U.S. Census Bureau, *Annual Survey of Public Pensions: State- and Locally-Administered Defined Benefit Data Summary Report: 2011* and the U.S. Department of Labor, *Private Pension Plan Bulletin. Table A1. Number of Pension Plans, Total Participants, Active Participants, Assets, Contributions, and Benefits, 2011.*

[2] See GAO, *State and Local Government Pension Plans: Economic Downturn Spurs Efforts to Address Costs and Sustainability,* GAO-12-322 (Washington, D.C.: Mar. 2, 2012).

[3] Pension liabilities can variously be referred to as "liabilities," "accrued liabilities," "funding targets," "obligations," or other terms, depending on the user of the term (e.g., actuaries, economists, accountants, lawyers) and the context and purpose of the measurement, as discussed later. Generally, such liabilities are reduced by the value of plan assets in evaluating the plans.

[4] A bond-based approach produces higher estimates of pension obligations because discount rates under this approach are generally lower than discount rates under the assumed-return approach. U.S. plans that use the assumed-return approach currently often use discount rates between 7 and 8 percent, based in part on historical returns or historical interest rates (these rates are nominal and not adjusted for inflation). See appendix III for GAO analysis of historical returns. Based on historical interest rates, there have been instances where discount rates under a bond-based approach, if used at the time, would likely have been higher than the assumed-return assumptions then in use. For example, from 1980 to 1985 the 30-year Treasury interest rate exceeded 10 percent. (See fig. 2 later in this report).

[5] By a "typical" plan, we mean a plan with a more or less average mix of workers and retirees. For example, one consulting firm publishes a bond yield curve and applies it to sample pension plans that it characterizes as "Retiree," "Mature," "Average,", and "Young." It describes the Average plan as having a typical mix of active workers and retirees. See, Mercer, *Mercer Pension Discount Yield Curve and Index Rates in the U.S.*, accessed on 9/8/14, http://www.mercer.com/insights/point/2014/mercer-pension-discount- yield-curve-an-index-rates-in-us.html. Pension plans that have projected benefit payout cash flows of long "duration" (e.g., closer to "Young" than to "Retiree") have liabilities that are more sensitive to changes in discount rates. Duration is a measure of the sensitivity of the present value of a series of cash flows to a change in the discount rate. It is related to the present-value-weighted average length of the cash flows.

[6] The "smoothing" of discount rates generally refers to the averaging of bond-based interest rates over multiple current and historical years.

[7] Please see appendix IV for a summary of each of these countries' DB systems and discounting practices.

[8] There are also some DB plans that are "cash balance" plans, which are a type of "hybrid" DB plan that expresses accrued benefits as hypothetical account balances, with benefits accruing annually based on a specified percentage of salary and interest earnings. Discount rate issues for "cash balance" plans, as well as other types of DB plans under which plan benefits are based in some part on the investment performance of plan assets, include additional considerations that are outside the scope of this report.

[9] However, previous GAO work suggests that separating participants in DC plans can also experience challenges. See GAO, *401(K) Plans: Labor and IRS Could Improve the Rollover Process for Participants,* GAO-13-30 (Washington, D.C.: Mar. 7, 2013).

[10] Single-employer plans include a category of plans known as multiple-employer plans, which should not be confused with multiemployer plans. Multiple-employer plans are typically established without collective bargaining agreements and can be either DB or DC. Multiple-employer DB plans must be funded as if each participating employer is funding a separate plan, and plan assets have to be allocated among separate accounts maintained for each employer-sponsor. In contrast, multiemployer plans are established through collective bargaining agreements between labor unions and two or more employers, and plan assets are maintained in a single account. For Internal Revenue Service purposes, multiple-employer plans are treated the same as single-employer plans. Relative to other single-employer plans, multiple-employer plans may provide advantages, such as pooling assets for investment purposes and reducing the cost of plan administration, to employers in certain trades or professions. See GAO, *Private Sector Pensions, Federal Agencies Should Collect Data and Coordinate of Multiple Employer Plans*, GAO-12-665 (Washington D.C.: Sept. 13, 2012).

[11] Our discussion about multiemployer plans will not cover the structure of the current multiemployer system and the challenges that it poses to many plans as it is outside the scope of this report. We discussed many of these issues in a prior report. See GAO, *Private Pensions: Timely Action Needed to Address Impending Multiemployer Plan Insolvencies*, GAO-13-240 (Washington D.C.: Mar. 28, 2013).

[12] For the rest of this report, "pension plan" or "plan" means, in the U.S. context, a "tax-qualified" DB plan. While the federal government sponsors DB plans for federal civilian and military employees, these plans were not within the scope of our work.

[13] Some types of plans are typically not insured by PBGC, such as those offered by professional service employers (such as doctors and lawyers) that have never had more than 25 active participants since the enactment date of ERISA, and those offered by church groups (unless the plan has elected to be covered), or plans of federal, state, or local governments.

[14] PBGC's single-employer and multiemployer insurance programs are maintained separately, each with a separate fund. In the multiemployer program, PBGC provides financial assistance in the form of loans to plans that become insolvent, that is, plans that do not have sufficient assets to pay pension benefits at PBGC's guaranteed level for a full plan year. Although such financial assistance is referred to as a "loan," and is by law required to be repaid, in practice such loans have almost never been repaid, as plans generally do not emerge from insolvency. Before PBGC will provide the loans, participants' retirement benefits must be reduced to a level specified in law. Even after insolvency, the plan remains an independent entity managed by its board of trustees. This contrasts with the agency's single-employer program under which PBGC does not provide financial assistance to ongoing plans, but instead takes over terminated underfunded plans as a trustee, and pays benefits directly to participants.

[15] The guaranteed benefit limits for participants in single-employer plans cannot exceed the statutory maximum, adjusted annually, at the time the plan terminates. For 2014, the maximum is about $59,320 per year for a person retiring at age 65 with no survivor benefit (that is, a single-life annuity); the maximum is indexed for inflation. The maximum is lower for those retiring under age 65, higher for those retiring over age 65, and lower for those with a survivor benefit. In addition, for any benefit increase implemented through a plan amendment that has been in effect for less than 5 years, only a pro-rata portion can be guaranteed. In contrast, the guaranteed benefit limits for participants in multiemployer plans are not indexed for inflation and do not vary with age at retirement, but do vary with a participant's years of service, For a participant with 30 years of service, PBGC fully insures the first $3,960 of a participant's annual benefit, plus three quarters of the next $11,880 of annual benefit, for a maximum annual payout of $12,870. For a participant with 10 years of service, this maximum annual payout is reduced to $4,290. If PBGC's multiemployer fund were to run out of money, PBGC would be unable to pay even these lower insured amounts. See GAOand PBGC, *FY 2013 PBGC Projections Report.*

[16] See GAOand GAO, *Pension Benefit Guaranty Corporation: Redesigned Premium Structure Could Better Align Rates with Risk from Plan Sponsors,* GAO-13-58 (Washington D.C.: Nov. 7, 2012).

[17] PBGC runs its single-employer simulation model under 5,000 possible future scenarios. A majority of the simulations project decreases in PBGC's single-employer deficit. PBGC, *FY 2013 PBGC Projections Report.*

[18] These projections are based on 500 simulations of the economy and plan sponsor behavior. See PBGC, *FY 2013 PBGC Projections Report.*

[19] According to PBGC, in the event that the multiemployer insurance fund is exhausted, affected participants then relying on the PBGC pension guarantee would receive an extremely small fraction of what PBGC guarantees or, potentially, nothing. According to PBGC officials, once the insurance fund's cash balance is depleted, the agency would have to rely solely on the annual insurance premium receipts. The precise effect that the insolvency of the multiemployer insurance fund would have on retirees receiving the PBGC guaranteed

benefit depends on a number of factors—primarily the number of guaranteed benefit recipients and PBGC's annual premium income at that time. GAO.

[20] For the same period, there were about 19 million state and local government employees and over 106 million private sector employees. See U.S. Department of Labor, U.S. Bureau of Labor Statistics, *National Compensation Survey: Employee Benefits in the United States, March 2013* (Washington, D.C.: Sept. 2013).

[21] See GAO, *State and Local Government Retiree Benefits: Current Status of Benefit Structures, Protections, and Fiscal Outlook for Funding Future Costs,* GAO-07-1156 (Washington D.C.: Sept. 24, 2007).

[22] See 42 U.S.C. § 410(a)(7). Historically, Social Security did not require coverage of state and local government employment. As a result, some state and local government workers who were not covered by a retirement system were left without benefits when they retired. To help these employees, in 1950 section 218 was added to the Social Security Act allowing states to enter into voluntary agreements to provide Social Security coverage to certain state and local government employees not covered by public pension plans. Social Security Act Amendments of 1950, Pub. L. No. 81-734, § 106, 64 Stat. 477, 514 (codified at 42 U.S.C. § 218). In 1954, voluntary coverage was extended to those already covered by plans as well. Social Security Amendments of 1954, Pub. L. No. 83-761, § 101(h)(2), 68 Stat. 1052, 1056 (codified at 42 U.S.C. § 218(d)(3)). Starting in 1991, the Social Security Act generally required all state and local government employees to be covered by Social Security if they were not already covered by a state or local retirement system. Revenue Reconciliation Act of 1990, Pub. L. No. 101-508, § 11332, 104 Stat. 1388-469. See GAO, *Social Security Administration: Management Oversight Needed to Ensure Accurate Treatment of State and Local Government Employees*, GAO-10-938 (Washington, D.C.: Sept. 29, 2010) and GAO-12-322.

[23] GAO

[24] To further clarify the difference between government and private sector pension plans, the Internal Revenue Service issued an advance notice of proposed rulemaking in November 2011 relating to the definition of the term "governmental plan." The regulation under consideration is intended to establish coordinated criteria for determining whether a plan is a governmental plan and address current uncertainty regarding entities with organizational, regulatory, and contractual connections with states or political subdivisions of states. Determination of Governmental Plan Status, 76 Fed. Reg. 69,172 (Nov. 8, 2011) (to be codified at 26 C.F.R. pt. 1). The rule has not been finalized.

[25] Committee on Ways and Means, Private Pension Tax Reform, H.R. Rep. No. 12855 (1974).

[26] Employer contributions to qualified pension plans that meet certain requirements— whether defined benefit or defined contribution—are generally not counted as taxable income to employees when the contributions are made. However, when pension benefits are paid, amounts not previously taxed are subject to federal and perhaps state tax. This also applies to the interest income such contributions generate. As an alternative, some state and local government qualified DC pension plans provide an option for designated contributions to Roth accounts, and such contributions to Roth accounts are made after taxation. The interest income earned on such contributions is generally not subject to tax upon distribution, provided that the requirements and restrictions applicable to such accounts under the Internal Revenue Code have been satisfied.

[27] Financial reporting standards are also sometimes referred to as accounting standards.

[28] Actuarial assumptions are needed to project the amount, likelihood, and timing of future benefits and to determine their present value, and include both economic and demographic assumptions. Economic assumptions typically include those for inflation, future salary increases, and the discount rate. Demographic assumptions typically include those for the likelihood of termination of employment, age of retirement, form of benefit elected, and longevity. Developing actuarial assumptions typically involves both the analysis of data and the application of professional judgment, and different actuaries might reach different

conclusions as to appropriate assumptions. In addition, depending on the type of assumption, the type of plan, and other circumstances, particular actuarial assumptions might be selected by the actuary, selected by the plan sponsor, or prescribed by statute or regulation. As a result of these factors (as well as the differences among conceptual approaches in the case of discount rates), actuarial assumptions can sometimes vary considerably among plans. Actuarial standards of practice include guidance on factors an actuary should consider when selecting an assumption or providing advice on selecting an assumption, as well as guidance on disclosures an actuary should make when assumptions are selected by others, including disclosures regarding the reasonableness of such assumptions.

[29] The pattern by which the liability builds up over an employee's career varies according to the "actuarial cost method," discussed later.

[30] "Normal cost" is also sometimes referred to as "service cost."

[31] These primary approaches in turn can have different variations, such as the use of "smoothing" with bond-based approaches, as is used by private sector single-employer plan sponsors under ERISA, where bond interest rates are averaged over multiple current and historical years.

[32] See GAO, *State and Local Government Pension Plans: Governance Practices and Long-term Investment Strategies Have Evolved Gradually as Plans Take On Increased Investment Risk*, GAO-10-754 (Washington, D.C.: Aug. 24, 2010). Discount rates as high as 8.5 percent have become less common in the interval since the publication of this report.

[33] Unless otherwise noted, discount rates and other interest rates cited in this report are nominal and not adjusted for the effects of inflation.

[34] This discount rate approach is also used in determining minimum funding requirements for multiemployer plans.

[35] We use the term "plan costs" generically, which can refer, depending on the context, to a plan's liability or normal cost, and to funding or financial reporting calculations, among other measures and purposes.

[36] The discount rate under this approach often will not be a single rate, but rather a "yield curve" of fixed income rates at multiple maturities.

[37] See later discussion for details on recent rates under some variations of the bond-based approach outlined here.

[38] The FASB accounting standards referenced throughout this report refer to requirements for plan sponsor, and not individual plan, financial reporting.

[39] Under ERISA, private sector single-employer sponsors are required to use a bond- based approach to determine the minimum required contribution. Within this framework, these sponsors have two options. Plan sponsors are given the option of using a full yield curve approach, which matches projected benefit payments to high-quality corporate bond interest rates as of a current or very recent month, so that under this option, the measurement of plan liabilities would be tied to current or very recent market conditions. A plan sponsor choosing this approach would discount a benefit payment due in 10 years at the yield curve rate as published by Treasury for year 10. However, single-employer plan sponsors may also elect to discount using a simplified three-segment yield curve published by Treasury, with the three different segment interest rates applicable to benefit payments due in less than 5 years, 5 to 20 years, and 20 years or more. Under the segment rate approach, the interest rates are based on a 2-year average of high-quality corporate bond rates but also cannot be higher or lower than maximum and minimum segment rates as set in law in 2012 as part of the Moving Ahead for Progress in the 21st Century Act (MAP-21).The MAP-21 maximum and minimum apply to plans that use the segment rate approach, and are based on long-term (25-year) historical bond averages. MAP-21's effect on discount rates is designed to be temporary. Because average interest rates over the past 25 years are significantly higher than more recent market rates, the MAP-21 changes have had the effect of significantly increasing ERISA discount rates over what they would otherwise have been,

thereby lowering measurements of plan liabilities and reducing minimum funding requirements. Legislation was signed in August 2014 that further extends the use of 25-year averaging of interest rates for determining minimum funding standards for private sector single-employer plans. Pub. L. No. 113-159, 128 Stat. 1839. Under either option, the market interest rates for any month, prior to any historical averaging, are based on an average of daily rates over the course of the month. Further, plan sponsors can elect to use rates as of an "applicable month," consistently applied from year to year, which can be the month containing the plan's annual valuation date or any of the preceding four months.

[40] *Report of the Blue Ribbon Panel on Public Pension Plan Funding: An Independent Panel Commission by the Society of Actuaries* (February 2014).

[41] A variation currently in use involves historical averaging of Treasury rates over recent years to determine a "current liability," an additional liability measure calculated for multiemployer plans. The discount rate for this purpose must be between 90 percent and 105 percent of a weighted average of interest rates on 30-year Treasury bonds over the prior 4 years. In the weighted average calculation, the most recent year is given a weight of 4, the next most recent year a weight of 3, the year before that a weight of 2, and the first year a weight of 1. The weighted average is calculated and published by Treasury.

[42] The "quality" of a bond refers to an assessment of its credit risk, or the ability of the bond issuer to fulfill its future contractual obligations. Typically, nationally recognized rating companies perform credit analysis on the issuing entity and issue their conclusions in the form of ratings. Bond issues are assigned a rating commensurate with their credit risk. Among corporate bonds, AAA/Aaa rated bonds are said to be "prime," or of the lowest credit risk, followed next by AA/Aa rated bonds which are of "high quality," and so on, with high yield, or "junk bonds," being the lowest quality or of the highest credit risk. Generally, the yield, or return on a bond, is inversely related to its credit risk, with risk-free Treasury bonds bearing the lowest yields and "junk bonds" the highest.

[43] PBGC's discount rate is based on interest rate factors that are specifically developed such that, when combined with PBGC's longevity assumptions, will approximate single- premium nonparticipating group annuity purchase rates. PBGC obtains information about the prices charged by private life insurers from quarterly surveys conducted for PBGC by the American Council of Life Insurers (ACLI). The ACLI surveys gather group annuity pricing information as of March 31, June 30, September 30, and December 31 of each year. The surveys collect information on private-sector group annuity prices for immediate and deferred annuities at a range of ages. These prices are net of administrative expenses: that is, the prices exclude costs for record-keeping, communication with annuitants, related corporate overhead, etc., but include profit and taxes. Using data from the annuity survey, PBGC determines two interest factors to compute estimates of the present value of its liabilities — a "select" factor to discount projected payouts for an initial period of years and an "ultimate" factor to discount projected payouts thereafter.

[44] Bonds are generally priced based upon the present value of their expected cash flows and the yield, or interest rate, which is commensurate with other bonds of comparable maturity and credit quality. Annuities, generally offered by life insurance companies that would typically guarantee lifetime streams of benefit payments to beneficiaries, are priced with regard to current market or bond-based interest rates but also typically include the addition of various fees, which include the insurer's administrative and marketing expenses, the cost of capital and surplus, and profit to the insurer. Additionally, annuity pricing typically includes allowance for longevity and other demographic risks. These differences generally result in annuity prices being higher than pension liabilities calculated based on high-quality bond rates (i.e., in implied annuity interest rates that are lower than high-quality bond interest rates). In addition, the spreads between implied annuity interest rates and high-quality bond interest rates will vary over time, just as the spreads among various classes of corporate bonds and Treasury bonds will vary over time. The actual market price of an annuity can depend on many factors, including the duration of the liabilities expected to be settled, the

size of the purchase, the average pension amount for the pensions being purchased, capital market conditions, and competitive pressures in the group annuity market at the time of purchase.

45 The only risk that would remain would be the solvency of the insurance company itself. The U.S. insurance industry is generally regulated at the state level. Solvency protections include capital standards and state guaranty funds. See GAO, *Insurance Markets: Impacts of and Regulatory Response to the 2007-2009 Financial Crisis*, GAO-13-583 (Washington D.C.: June 27, 2013).

46 As a result, it is often the case that a private sector single-employer plan sponsor's valuation of its pension liabilities under FASB or ERISA requirements is lower than PBGC's valuation of that same plan.

47 For a discussion of different perspectives on PBGC's discount rate and the measurement of its liabilities and deficit, see *American Academy of Actuaries Issue Brief: Perspectives on the PBGC Single-Employer Deficit* (August 2013).

48 As discussed, a variation on the bond-based approach is to use an historical average of bond interest rates over some period preceding the measurement date. Because of declines in interest rates over recent years and decades, use of an historical average of interest rates can, depending on the averaging period, result in discount rates that are significantly in excess of current market interest rates. Experts who supported a bond- based approach to setting discount rates typically disagreed with the use of extended historical averages, and sometimes with any averaging at all.

49 Our categorization of discount rates into two broad categories, "assumed-return" and "bond-based," along with the subcategories of variations under "bond-based," is constructed for the purpose of illustrating certain key characteristics of different approaches. It is not the only way to group the various approaches, and other experts might do so differently. For example, one expert felt that annuity settlement rates should be placed into a separate third category rather than grouping it with bond-based approaches. This expert also viewed the ERISA / PPA / MAP-21 approach of relying on a 25-year historical average of bond rates as not being "bond-based" because of its remoteness from current or recent bond rates. The key factor underlying our categorization is that under the assumed-return approach, the discount rate depends on the allocation of plan assets; this is not the case for any of the bond-based variations that we identified, which depend on characteristics of a plan's liabilities but not on the assets set aside to finance them.

50 In a prefunded plan, a sponsor makes contributions that go into a trust fund, grow with investment returns, and eventually are paid out as benefits at a later date.

51 According to Canadian experts with whom with spoke, each province has its own regulatory body for pension plans under its jurisdiction (with the exception of Prince Edward Island). At the federal level, the Office of the Superintendent of Financial Institutions (OSFI) regulates and supervises private pension plans in federally regulated areas of employment and certain enumerated public plans. One expert added that there are many national companies in provincially regulated businesses such as retail, manufacturing, and oil. In these plans, benefit standards are dictated by the rules of the province of employment, while other considerations that are of a plan-wide nature, such as the funding rules, are governed by the rules of the province with the plurality of plan members.

52 However, experts told us that funding relief measures provided in recent years have varied across provinces. Experts also told us that Quebec has many differences in pension regulation compared to the rest of Canada.

53 With the exception of Ontario province, which has pension insurance that insures a nominal benefit of up to one thousand Canadian dollars per month, experts noted that there is no pension insurance program in Canada.

54 The DNB examines the financial position of pension funds and regulates the discount rates. The Netherlands Authority for the Financial Markets (AFM) monitors market conduct relating to pension funds' obligations to provide information to members.

[55] Funded status is a comparison of plan assets to plan liabilities. One measure of funded status is the "funded ratio," which is calculated by dividing plan assets by plan liabilities. Another measure of funded status is the difference between plan assets and plan liabilities, that is, the dollar amount of surplus or deficit. For example, if assets are greater than liabilities, the funded ratio is greater than 100 percent and the plan has a surplus (overfunding) equal to the excess of assets over liabilities; if liabilities are greater than assets, the funded ratio is less than 100 percent and the plan has a deficit (underfunding, or unfunded liability) equal to the excess of liabilities over assets.

[56] In the Netherlands, pension plan trustees can decide to increase benefits for wage or price inflation ("indexation") if the funded ratio is sufficiently high. If the funded ratio stays below a minimum funded ratio of 105 percent, accrued benefits can be reduced.

[57] For most public sector plans in the United Kingdom, benefits are paid out of general revenue. The discussion in this report about discount rate practices in the United Kingdom will be related primarily to private sector plans. Beginning in 2015, the U.K. Pensions Regulator will assume additional responsibility for regulating the governance and administration of public service pension plans.

[58] Participants of plans that become insolvent may be eligible for benefits from the Pension Protection Fund (PPF). The PPF is the U.K. equivalent to the U.S. Pension Benefit Guaranty Corporation. The main function of the PPF is to provide compensation to members of eligible defined benefit pension schemes when there is a qualifying insolvency event in relation to the employer, and where there are insufficient assets in the pension plan to cover the PPF level of compensation.

[59] In the United Kingdom, the term pension "scheme" is used rather than pension "plan," with no pejorative connotation.

[60] For public sector plans, one exception to the typical use of assumed return discount rates is that some plans use a fixed discount rate set by its jurisdiction, which might not necessarily be tied to how plan assets are invested.

[61] The minimum required contribution for multiemployer plans is generally based on a funding target using an assumed return discount rate. A second measure of liability, called the "current liability" and based on a 4-year weighted average of 30-year Treasury rates, is also reported by plans on Schedule MB of Form 5500. However, experts viewed multiemployer plans as operating primarily on an assumed return basis, although they had differing views of the significance of the current liability calculation (see footnote 109 later). The "current liability" can affect the minimum required contribution in certain years, and is used in determining the maximum tax-deductible contribution, but the minimum funding target remains the liability measured using an assumed return discount rate.

[62] FASB accounting standards for discounting are typically not applicable for participating employers in a multiemployer plan, in part because of presumed difficulties in reliably measuring an employer's share of the plan's total liability. However, the accounting requirements are applicable for individual plan reporting, which for a multiemployer plan are the same as those for private single-employer plans for individual plan reporting, noted below.

[63] Under current GASB standards, plan sponsors use an assumed-return approach. Under a new GASB standard with implementation required by fiscal years beginning after June 15, 2014, plan sponsors would use a blended approach which industry experts have indicated is likely to be closer to an assumed-return approach in most instances. See appendix II for more information.

[64] As noted, multiemployer plans calculate an additional liability measure under ERISA, called the current liability, based on a 4-year weighted average of 30-year Treasury rates. However, experts viewed multiemployer plans as operating primarily on an assumed return basis, although they had differing views of the significance of the current liability calculation (see footnote 109 later).

[65] For current workers, the effects of different actuarial cost methods also have to be taken into account in comparing the size of different liability measurements, as discussed later in this section and in appendix II.

[66] National Association of State Retirement Administrators, *NASRA Issue Brief: Public Pension Plan Investment Return Assumptions* (December 2013). Historically, private sector multiemployer plans have often used assumed return assumptions of 7.5 percent or higher. Between 1995 and 2007, large multiemployer plans used an average assumed return, weighted by plan liabilities, of 7.57 percent. For the 2010 plan year, multiemployer plans used an average assumed return, weighted by plan liabilities, of 7.52 percent. See Department of Labor, Department of the Treasury, and Pension Benefit Guaranty Corporation, *Multiemployer Pension Plans: Report to Congress Required by the Pension Protection Act of 2006* (Washington, D.C.: Jan. 22, 2013).

[67] As shown in table 1, private sector multiemployer plans also generally discount using the assumed-return approach for funding purposes under ERISA. All other assumptions and factors held constant, a private sector multiemployer plan discounting using an assumed-return approach would generally result in lower reported liabilities than a private sector single-employer plan with the same pension obligations discounting using a bond- based approach with little or no smoothing. For current workers, the difference may sometimes be lessened somewhat by differences in actuarial cost method.

[68] For current workers, this difference will typically be lessened somewhat by differences in actuarial cost method, discussed later in this section. 15, 2014, plan sponsors would use a blended approach which industry experts have indicated is likely to be closer to an assumed-return approach in most instances. See appendix II for more information.

[69] As discussed, under a variation of the bond-based approach, as advocated by some financial economists for certain purposes, the bond quality could be chosen to match the estimated riskiness of the pension promise. Under this approach, for example, a pension promise deemed highly risky might be discounted using interest rates on high-yield low- rated bonds, rates that could be closer to assumed returns used by public and private sector multiemployer plans than to high-quality corporate bond or Treasury rates. For some of the reasoning for and against this approach, see Financial Accounting Standards Board, *Statement of Financial Accounting Standards No. 157: Fair Value Measurements, paragraphs C47 to C49.*

[70] For example, historical averages of interest rates can be significantly different than current interest rates.

[71] Under ERISA standards, plan sponsors have two options—-whether to use historically averaged rates or more current market rates—-and within each option the specific rates are defined by law and published by Treasury. For private sector single-employer plan sponsors who elect to use historically averaged rates, under a simplified three-segment yield curve, the interest rates as prescribed by Treasury with respect to any month reflect the average, for the 24 month period ending with the month preceding such month, of monthly yields on investment grade corporate bonds with varying maturities and that are in the top 3 quality levels available (i.e., AAA, AA, and A). For private sector single- employer plan sponsors who elect to use more current market interest rates without historical averaging, the interest rates prescribed by Treasury, using a full yield curve approach, are determined in the same way as the rates used for the segment rate approach but without 24-month averaging. Under either option, the market interest rates for any month, prior to any historical averaging, are based on an average of daily rates over the course of the month. Further, plan sponsors can elect to use rates as of an "applicable month," consistently applied from year to year, which can be the month containing the plan's annual valuation date or any of the preceding four months.

[72] PBGC updates their interest rate factors on a quarterly basis based on surveys on annuity pricing information as of March 31, June 30, September 30, and December 31st of each year. Comparisons among market-based (i.e., without smoothing) interest rate factors, such

as between PBGC discount rates and rates that might be used for private sector single-employer sponsor financial reporting, will vary at different points in time and could change based on market conditions affecting interest rate spreads and other factors. Additionally, discount rates based on annuity pricing will account for mortality and other risks that are not incorporated into a corporate bond index. For example, the American Academy of Actuaries reported that, based on the annuity quotes obtained for the federal fiscal year ended September 30, 2012, the PBGC discount rate was 3.28 percent, based on a liability duration of approximately 11 years, while the Citigroup Pension Liability index as of the same date, which reflects high-quality corporate bond yields (rated no lower than AA), was 3.9 percent based on a liability duration of approximately 20 years. Adjusting the Citigroup index to a duration comparable to PBGC's would reduce the interest rate to about 3.5 percent, much closer to PBGC's rate. For details, see *American Academy of Actuaries Issue Brief: Perspectives on the PBGC Single-Employer Deficit* (August 2013).

[73] An actuarial cost method is a method for allocating retirement costs among employees' working years. Those costs allocated to past service become part of the accrued liability; those costs allocated to future service become part of future normal costs. Prescribed actuarial cost methods vary among GASB, ERISA, and FASB. In appendix II, we discuss cost methods allowed under GASB, ERISA, and FASB.

[74] The differences in liabilities resulting from the use of differing actuarial cost methods between public sector and private sector single-employer plan sponsors only apply to the liability for current employees. For retired annuitants and separated deferred annuitants, most actuarial cost methods result in the same level of liability. Thus, if a plan has a large proportion of retirees and/or separated deferred annuitants, it becomes even more likely that the differences among actuarial cost methods are less significant than the differences in discount rates.

[75] Under ERISA's single-employer standards, while plan sponsors may elect from two options (for example, whether to use historically averaged rates or more current market rates), within each option the specific rates are defined by law and published by Treasury.

[76] FASB standards require discount rates to reflect the rate at which pension benefits could be effectively settled. In estimating these "settlement rates," plan sponsors have discretion in interpreting and applying this requirement. They can look either at available information about rates implicit in the pricing of current annuity contracts or interest rates on high-quality bonds that are currently and expected to be available that match the duration of the pension benefits; in practice, discount rates derived from high-quality bonds are typically used. Because current bond rates are observable in the market, there are fairly narrow limits to how much a FASB discount rate can vary and still be considered reasonable. Jon Waite, *Pension Accounting Research Series. 2013: An Update for Disclosures for 2012* (SEI Institutional Group, 2012).

[77] The incentive to invest in riskier assets could also apply to private sector multiemployer plans because they generally use the assumed-return approach for minimum funding purposes.

[78] Pension obligation bonds are taxable general obligation bonds issued by the public plan sponsor. The money received for these bonds is designated for investment in the pension trust. As a result, a pension obligation is replaced by a long-term fixed obligation of the government issuing the bond. As GAO has previously reported, some states have issued pension obligation bonds to address severe plan underfunding. Pension obligation bonds had been an attractive option for some governments because interest rates and borrowing costs were considered low and pension assets invested in equities allowed plan sponsors to assume future returns that were higher than the cost of borrowing. See GAO-10-754.

[79] There are various legal constraints on the ability of plan sponsors to reduce future or current benefit accruals, which vary further for public and private sector plans.

[80] GAO

[81] The bond-based discount rate for funding purposes under ERISA includes the option to use rates that are based on a 24-month average of interest rates, further bounded by rates tied to

a very long (25-year) smoothing period that would be less likely to create an incentive to invest in bonds. The bond-based discount rate for financial reporting purposes under FASB is based on current market interest rates.

82 However, from the standpoint of financial economics theory, the "risk-adjusted cost" would be the same under both the low-risk and high-risk financing approaches. The risk- adjusted cost takes into account the market price for bearing risk.

83 For example, Actuarial Standard of Practice No. 4 cites the following examples of measurement purposes: periodic costs, actuarially determined contribution requirements, benefit provision pricing, comparability assessments, withdrawal liabilities, benefit plan settlements, funded status assessments, market value assessments, and plan sponsor mergers and acquisitions.

84 Two experts suggested that a liability measurement using an assumed-return approach for this purpose would be better labeled a "funding target" rather than a "liability."

85 Public sector plan sponsors do not always make the full contributions determined by their funding calculations. See GAO

86 As noted earlier, this only applies to tax qualified plans.

87 However, ERISA's bond-based approach is currently bounded by 25-year historical averages. See appendix II for more information. In general, multiemployer plan liability calculations are more similar to public plan liability calculations than to private sector single-employer plan calculations because the first two generally use an assumed-return approach and the last generally uses a bond-based approach, albeit with significant smoothing.

88 U.S. Department of Labor, Employee Benefits Security Administration, *Private Pension Plan Bulletin: Abstract of 2011 Form 5500 Annual Reports* (June 2013).

89 Reporting plan liabilities to different stakeholders can be done via other venues besides financial reports, such as in a published actuarial report. Actuarial reports are prepared by the plan actuary and are typically submitted on an annual basis to the plan sponsor or regulating entity. An independent panel commissioned by the Society of Actuaries recently recommended that actuarial reports for public pension plans provide expanded disclosures, including additional risk analysis and multiple liability measures, and that plan sponsors share these reports in a timely manner with elected and civil service officials as well as other parties of interest, including taxpayers and service recipients, plan member and union officials, other stakeholders, and the media. *Report of the Blue Ribbon Panel on Public Pension Plan Funding: An Independent Panel Commission by the Society of Actuaries* (February 2014).

90 Jon Waite, *Pension Accounting Research Series 2013: An Update for Disclosures for 2012* (SEI Institutional Group, 2012).

91 Under GASB standards governmental entities are generally considered "going- concerns." Under current GASB standards, plan sponsors use an assumed-return approach. Under a new GASB standard with implementation required by fiscal years beginning after June 15, 2014, plan sponsors would use a blended approach, which industry experts have indicated is likely to be closer to an assumed-return approach in most instances. See appendix II for more detailed information about new GASB pension accounting standards going into effect. Due to differences in actuarial cost methods between FASB and GASB standards, the difference in the value of liabilities under GASB standards compared to the bond-based approach under FASB standards may be somewhat less than the differences in discount rates may otherwise suggest.

92 As noted earlier, for some of the reasoning for and against this approach, see Financial Accounting Standards Board, *Statement of Financial Accounting Standards No. 157: Fair Value Measurements, paragraphs C47 to C49.*

93 Plans can also offer participants lump sums that are based on IRS-published rates for high-quality corporate bonds.

[94] This is often the case even though the measure disclosed under FASB standards, known as the projected benefit obligation, or PBO, includes a projection of future salary increases, whereas a solvency measure generally does not.

[95] For the investment risk to actually be minimized, the plan assets would actually have to be invested in such Treasury bonds using a portfolio of Treasury bonds that matched the expected timing of benefit payments. As noted, a panel commissioned by the Society of Actuaries recommended that public plans disclose an additional liability measurement using this method, and at least one public plan currently discloses such a supplemental measure. *Report of the Blue Ribbon Panel on Public Pension Plan Funding: An Independent Panel Commission by the Society of Actuaries* (February 2014).

[96] GAO is engaged in a review of "risk transfer" strategies, such as offering lump sums to participants, employed by private pension plan sponsors to reduce the risks associated with sponsoring defined benefit plans. A report is expected to be issued in late 2014.

[97] ERISA minimum lump sum calculations are determined based on 26 U.S.C. § 417(e)(3), which specifies the interest rate and mortality assumptions plan sponsors must use in calculating the minimum amount of any lump-sum offers for tax-qualified pension plans. These minimum lump sum amounts vary depending on the form and amount of a participant's promised benefit and age.

[98] Financial economic theory (or financial economics) is a subset of microeconomics, largely devoted to the study of capital markets. Financial economic theory informs the premise of certain bond-based approaches: that the promise to make a future payment of benefits is similar to a promise to pay off any other kind of debt (such as a bond) and should be valued in a similar way. The theory also says that the discount rate should not be related to a plan's asset al.location, but that it should be based on an external market measure of the value of future dollars today.

[99] "Costs" can refer to funding costs or financial reporting costs, either of which could be important to a plan sponsor. Conceptually, either type of cost will typically consist of a normal cost and an amortization of any unfunded liability, so that the cost will also depend on the length of the amortization period. Further, some "smoothing" could be used, either by smoothing the measurements of plan assets or liabilities (smoothing the inputs into the cost calculation) or by smoothing the output of the cost calculation. ERISA, FASB, and GASB have different rules for determining annual costs, which are outside the scope of this report. Sponsors will also be concerned about the volatility of the unfunded liability, not just the volatility of annual cost.

[100] As discussed, based on historical interest rates, there have been instances where discount rates under the bond-based approach may have been higher than the assumed long-term average rate of return. For example, from 1980 to 1985 the 30-year Treasury interest rate exceeded 10 percent. (See fig. 2 earlier.)

[101] The costs determined by the bond-based approach are more volatile than the assumed-return approach because for the bond-based approach (without smoothing) the practitioner is using market interest rates as of the measurement date of the calculation. Conversely, the costs determined by the assumed-returned approach, as practiced in the United States, have been more stable because the practitioner uses the rate of return that they believe can be returned on assets invested over the long term, informed at least in part by long-term historical averages. Long-term return assumptions used for U.S. plans have shown much more stability from year to year than market interest rates.

[102] This approach was proposed by the American Academy of Actuaries Pension Practice Council in a letter to conferees in May 2012 regarding the Pension Funding Stabilization provisions in the Moving Ahead for Progress in the 21st Century Act (MAP-21). The Academy suggested that directly smoothing contribution requirements (rather than smoothing discount rates) would preserve reported funded status and provide a clear and transparent measurement of contribution reductions.

[103] ERISA allows private sector plans to smooth their discount rates by allowing private sector single-employer plan sponsors to choose a 2-year average of bond rates. Since 2012, as part of MAP-21, this average is now based on long-term (25-year) bond averages. MAP-21's effect on discount rates is designed to be temporary, though legislation signed in August 2014 extends its effect. Because average interest rates over the past 25 years are significantly higher than more recent market rates, the MAP-21 changes had the effect of significantly increasing ERISA discount rates over what they would otherwise have been, thereby lowering measurements of plan liabilities and reducing minimum funding requirements and potentially putting plan participants and PBGC at greater risk.

[104] GAO

[105] One viewpoint is that a termination or solvency measurement for public plans is irrelevant because these plans are going-concerns, and the need for them to transfer their pension obligations to a third party (such as an insurance company) is remote, especially for plans that are fully-funded. An alternative viewpoint is that a solvency or low-risk measurement is useful for identifying the full cost of benefits without passing on risk to future taxpayers, users of public services, and plan participants.

[106] This perspective that a weak sponsor needs to use a lower discount rate is most applicable for funding purposes. (See later discussion of the use of this perspective in the United Kingdom.) In contrast, as noted earlier, for financial reporting and certain other purposes, some supporters of the bond-based approach argue that the bond quality used to discount liabilities should vary with the riskiness of the benefit promise, such that a weak plan sponsor of an underfunded plan would use a higher rate than a strong sponsor of the same plan, to reflect the risk of non-payment of the benefit promise. This would result in a weak sponsor reporting a lower liability than a stronger sponsor with a comparable plan. For some of the reasoning for and against this approach, see Financial Accounting Standards Board, *Statement of Financial Accounting Standards No. 157: Fair Value Measurements, paragraphs C47 to C49.*

[107] For example, an aging or maturing plan, such as a frozen plan over time, may be more vulnerable to "sequence of return risk" than a growing plan. This risk refers to the variability of investment performance over time, rather than a uniform average rate of return for the same period. Due to net cash outflows from benefit payments to retirees, a maturing plan has a diminishing asset base that can be particularly at risk if the plan encounters periods of low returns, as it will have less time to recover from the downturn, and less money to benefit from a future market upturn. The extent of the sequence of return risk depends on several factors, including the variability of returns, investment time horizon, and amount of money available for investment. See appendix III for the results of modeling the cash flows of hypothetical pension plans that illustrate the effects of plan characteristics on actual investment returns.

[108] Under the new GASB standard required for public pension plan sponsors for fiscal years beginning after June 15, 2014, state and local government plan sponsors will be required to disclose the sensitivity of their net pension liability calculation using discount rates that are 1 percent higher and 1 percent lower than the discount rate actually being used (a similar requirement applies under GASB's new standard for financial reporting by the plans themselves, for fiscal years beginning after June 15, 2013). This information would help interested financial report users to calculate estimates of the pension liability at alternative discount rates (although the accuracy of the estimate can diminish for large differences in discount rates). GASB cited the significance of the discount rate as motivating this new requirement. Some respondents to GASB's exposure draft would have gone further and required direct disclosure of additional measures of pension liability. In addition, the panel commissioned by the Society of Actuaries to report on public pension plan funding recommended that additional information be provided to all interested parties, such as through the actuary's report that is typically provided to plan trustees. The recommended additional information includes the plan liability calculated using a risk-free discount rate

(such as with a U.S. Treasury yield curve); a projection of future annual plan benefit payments, which would allow a user to calculate a liability at alternative discount rates with precision; and the results of specific stress testing.

[109] While this current liability measure could be accessed by stakeholders through the Department of Labor's Form 5500 database, some experts noted that this measure is generally not otherwise reported in certain other important communications. For example, they noted that it is not required to be reported in the Annual Funding Notice to plan participants, nor is it used in the annual certification of a multiemployer plan's "zone status," which is based on the funded status of the plan and determines whether remedial measures are necessary to improve the financial health of the plan (see GAO). However, other experts noted that the current liability measure is generally contained in the actuary's valuation report, and one expert stated that many actuarial valuation reports now show five or six measures of funded status, and that plan trustees are aware of these alternative measures. On the other hand, one expert noted that the use of a 4-year weighted average for the discount rate used in calculating the current liability measure, rather than a more current rate, limited its usefulness as a market-based liability measure. In addition, plans have a certain amount of discretion in selecting this current liability discount rate from within a range of 90 percent to 105 percent of this 4-year weighted average, and another expert noted that this discretion in choosing this rate limited its usefulness in making comparisons across plans.

[110] This assumes recent or current market conditions where bond-based discount rates have generally been lower than assumed-returns. As discussed, based on historical interest rates, there have been instances where discount rates under the bond-based approach may have been higher than the assumed long-term average rate of return. For example, from 1980 to 1985 the 30-year Treasury interest rate exceeded 10 percent. (See fig. 2 earlier.)

[111] Some advocates of multiple measures argued that such analysis alone is insufficient.

[112] Figure 3 is a simplification meant to illustrate some of the lines of argument but does not encompass all the views of the experts we interviewed, or capture all of the nuances of the various views such as the use of risk-free vs. other interest rates in the bond-based approach.

[113] According to the Public Fund Survey conducted by the National Association of State Retirement Administrators and the National Council on Teacher Retirement in 2013, 107 of the 126 plans surveyed used discount rates between 7.5 and 8 percent. National Association of State Retirement Administrators, *NASRA Issue Brief: Public Pension Plan Investment Return Assumptions* (April 2014). Historically, private sector multiemployer plans have often used assumed return assumptions of 7.5 percent or higher. Between 1995 and 2007, large multiemployer plans used an average assumed return, weighted by plan liabilities, of 7.57 percent. For the 2010 plan year, multiemployer plans used an average assumed return, weighted by plan liabilities, of 7.52 percent. See Department of Labor, Department of the Treasury, and Pension Benefit Guaranty Corporation, *Multiemployer Pension Plans: Report to Congress Required by the Pension Protection Act of 2006* (Washington, D.C.: Jan. 22, 2013).

[114] In addition, historical returns are not relevant in the context of a bond-based approach to discount rates, since the bond-based approach relies on observable market interest rates.

[115] GAO did not conduct an independent legal analysis to verify the information provided about the laws, regulations, or policies of the foreign countries selected for this study.

[116] Either of the two liabilities resulting from the bond-based or assumed-return approach could be higher than the other because of differences in actuarial cost method regarding whether the effect of projected future salary increases (for salary-based benefit formulas) received by plans' covered workforce is included in the liability.

[117] As discussed, a plan has an unfunded liability or is underfunded when its liabilities are greater than assets, so that the funded ratio is less than 100 percent. The amount of the unfunded liability is equal to the excess of liabilities over assets.

[118] A margin for adverse deviation is a provision that can be applied to an actuarial assumption in a manner that produces higher cost, or lower revenue, than a best-estimate assumption in order to provide a margin of safety against the risk that actual experience proves to be less favorable than the best-estimate assumption. For example, if the best- estimate of future investment returns is 7 percent and a margin for adverse deviation of 0.5 percent is applied, then the assumed return net of the margin would be 6.5 percent.

[119] Generally, plans in the Netherlands use the Euro rate swap curve to discount pension liabilities. A swap rate yield curve is a commonly used interest rate benchmark. The Euro swap curve is an interest rate benchmark that uses the Euro Interbank Offered Rate as the reference rate. The Euro Interbank Offered Rate is the rate at which bank deposits in countries that have adopted the Euro currency and are members of the European Union are offered by one prime bank to another prime bank. The actual swap rate for a given maturity is the fixed interest rate that is paid by the fixed rate counterparty in an interest rate swap transaction. In this report, the Netherlands' use of the Euro swap curve to discount pension liabilities is also referred to as a bond-based approach. See later discussion and appendix IV for more details on discount rate practices in the Netherlands.

[120] Generally, solvency requirements exist to mitigate the risk that benefits cannot be paid due to plan underfunding. This contrasts with going-concern risk which is the risk that a plan sponsor will go bankrupt.

[121] As we previously reported, the United Kingdom established a new risk-based pensions regulator in 2005 after a review of the previous regulator revealed inefficiencies with the compliance-based approach. See GAO, *Defined Contribution Plans: Approaches in Other Countries Offer Beneficial Strategies in Several Areas,* GAO-12-328 (Washington, D.C.: Mar. 22, 2012).

[122] The regulator also uses a risk-based approach in selecting which plans to investigate in detail each year. Under the "risk-based" approach, the regulator allocates resources based on an assessment that prioritizes risks in the context of its statutory objectives and focuses on the areas where it determines its actions will likely have the greatest effect.

[123] The Canadian Institute of Actuaries' standards of practice and regulators (such as Ontario and the Office of the Superintendent of Financial Institutions) do not prescribe a discount rate approach for the going-concern liability measurement. Experts told us that in practice, plans generally use the assumed-return approach for the going-concern liability measurement.

[124] More specifically, the required contribution is the sum of "normal cost" on a going- concern basis plus the larger of two different amortization calculations, a going-concern amortization and a solvency amortization. Normal cost is the cost of future benefits attributable to the current year of employees' service. The going-concern amortization is an amortization of the unfunded going-concern liability, with various components of the unfunded liability having remaining amortization periods of 15 years or less. The solvency amortization is an amortization of the unfunded solvency liability over 5 years.

[125] Although, as one expert noted, the solvency measure is also required in Ontario, which does have a pension insurance program that insures a nominal benefit of up to one thousand Canadian dollars (Can$1,000) per month.

[126] Upon the wind-up of a plan, retired members and retirement-eligible members will typically elect immediate annuities. Active members and members with deferred benefits may elect a lump sum , although the lump sum would have to go into an IRA-type of account that one expert described as "locked in," with limited exceptions for withdrawal. Certain aspects of the solvency measure can vary across regulators.

[127] The formula specifies a two-tier discount rate, with one discount rate applied to projected benefits that would have been paid in the first 10 years after the valuation date, and the second discount rate applied to projected benefits that would have been paid beyond 10 years after the valuation date. The formula was intended to approximate the results that would be obtained from discounting using a full yield curve based on highly rated provincial bonds.

[128] The Canadian Institute of Actuaries provides guidance related to establishing appropriate assumptions regarding the market price of immediate and deferred annuities for DB plan solvency valuations. In its guidance for plans with valuation dates between December 31, 2013 and December 30, 2014, the Canadian Institute of Actuaries estimated that the cost of purchasing non-indexed annuities could range from 50 to 80 basis points (depending on the duration of the liabilities) above Government of Canada bonds with maturities over 10 years. As of December 31, 2013, this would result in discount rates ranging from 3.63 to 3.93 percent.

[129] In addition, one expert noted that Canadian multiemployer plans tended to use shorter time periods to amortize unfunded liabilities than their U.S. counterparts, with typical Canadian amortization periods ranging from 8 to 12 years, depending on the province.

[130] The actuarial cost method used is unit credit (i.e., based on service and salary to date, with no projection of future salary increase). The liability also does not include future inflation-indexation of benefits.

[131] As mentioned, plans in the Netherlands generally use the Euro rate swap curve to discount pension liabilities. A DNB official told us that 3 month smoothing is a temporary measure to mitigate day-to-day interest rate volatility while more comprehensive changes to the system are contemplated. A DNB official told us that under future regulations, all policy decisions will be based on a 12 month moving average of the funding ratio.

[132] Prior to the introduction of this predetermined rate, called the Ultimate Forward Rate, pension plans discounted their liabilities using the full Euro rate swap curve as prescribed by the DNB. Before DNB introduced the use of market interest rates to discount pension liabilities in 2007, pension plans in the Netherlands determined the value of their liabilities using a maximum discount rate of 4 percent.

[133] A forward rate is a rate of interest for a future period that would equate the total return of a long-term bond with that of a strategy of rolling over shorter-term bonds. The forward rate is inferred from a yield curve.

[134] Plans can attempt to provide inflation-indexed benefits by investing in riskier asset portfolios, but the benefit increases are only granted to the extent they are supported by investment returns.

[135] An official told us that a common asset al.location of 50 percent equity, 40 percent bond, and 10 percent real estate would require a plan to be 120 percent funded, based on a 2.5 percent probability of shortfall in a one-year horizon. See appendix IV for more details on plan funding standards in the Netherlands.

[136] For example, using maximum return assumptions of 7 percent for equities and 4.2 percent for bonds (the current predetermined maximum bond-based discount rate as introduced by the DNB), a static portfolio allocation of 60 percent in equities and 40 percent in bonds would result in a composite assumed return of about 5.9 percent. The actual composite assumed return could be even lower since the portfolio may contain shorter duration bonds which would likely yield less than 4.2 percent under current conditions.

[137] In the Netherlands, there are two types of recovery plans based on different minimum funding targets that are commensurate with the riskiness of plan investments. According to officials we spoke with, plans with funded ratios less than the 105 percent base funding target must submit a recovery plan to return to this target within 3 years. Plans with funded ratios less than the risk-adjusted funding targets must submit a recovery plan to return to these targets within 15 years. In 2008, the recovery period for plans under the base funding threshold was extended by the government from 3 to 5 years as a vast majority of plans had to file recovery plans. As of July 2013, the regulator told us that there are still 70 plans in recovery status in this, the fifth year. In response, the regulator is in the process of contemplating more comprehensive changes to the pension regulatory system.

[138] The relevant regulation states that "the rates of interest used to discount future payments of benefits must be chosen prudently, taking into account either or both–(i) the yield on assets

held by the scheme to fund future benefits and the anticipated future investment returns, and (ii) the market redemption yields on government or other high- quality bonds."

139 Officials indicated that the U.K. parliament has established a new objective within the regulatory framework: to minimize any adverse impact on the sustainable growth of an employer when dealing with plan funding issues. Pursuant to this objective, in all its regulatory actions and guidance to trustees, the Pensions Regulator must now balance the financial position of the employer plan sponsor, especially regarding their ability to grow, with plan funding considerations.

140 These ratings of financial strength of plan sponsor companies by the Pensions Regulator are not made public.

141 Another important risk factor is plan asset al.location. One expert told us that the Pensions Regulator does not have direct jurisdiction over a plan's asset al.location, but if a plan invested too aggressively, the regulator would engage the plan trustees and use the regulatory powers it did have, such as reviewing the reasonability of plan contribution determinations, to try to persuade the plan trustees to adjust the level of risk.

142 Another official indicated that while discount rates for calculating liabilities must be chosen prudently, recovery plans could assume something closer to best estimate returns. The recovery plan does not change the calculation of the liability.

143 The average recovery plan length based on plans with valuation dates from September 22, 2010, to September 21, 2011, was 7.5 years.

144 In practice, an official suggested that the use of different discount rates for benefits for current and retired workers might reflect the different investment approaches used to finance these different components of plan liabilities, with plan assets allocated to high- quality bonds to back benefits for retired workers in pay status, and a portion of plan assets allocated to riskier, but potentially higher yielding investments, such as equities, to fund benefits for current workers not yet in pay status. In this sense, this "different rates" approach can be thought of as an assumed-return approach. We did not examine plan asset al.locations across countries. The regulator also told us that, increasingly, plans are using a yield-curve approach to discounting. This approach discounts projected plan benefit payments using interest rates on the yield curve that are approximated or matched to the timing of those benefit payments.

145 These figures were based on valuations for plans in recovery submitted to the regulator between 2005 and 2012.

146 Private plans are generally required to submit actuarial valuations to the regulator on a triennial basis with valuation dates from September 22 of one year to September 21 of the next year. The average discount rate for plans in deficit for the 7 valuation periods ending between 2006 and 2012 were: 5.2 percent in 2006, 5.5 percent in 2007, 5.7 percent in 2008, 5.3 percent in 2009, 5.3 percent in 2010, 5.3 percent in 2011, and 4.3 percent in 2012.

147 Many U.K. public plans used the Superannuation Contributions Adjusted for Past Experience discount rate to value their pension liabilities and set contributions. In response to concerns from an independent commission that the Superannuation Contributions Adjusted for Past Experience rate was higher than warranted, the U.K. government in 2011 announced that the discount rate used to calculate unfunded public pension contributions will be based on long term expectations of U.K. Gross Domestic Product growth, and a discount rate of 3 percent above the U.K. Consumer Prices Index was adopted. As of December 2013, the annual U.K. Consumer Prices Index was 2 percent, resulting in a 5 percent discount rate.

148 According to the Public Fund Survey conducted by the National Association of State Retirement Administrators and the National Council on Teacher Retirement in 2013, 107 of the 126 plans surveyed used discount rates between 7.5 and 8 percent. National Association of State Retirement Administrators, *NASRA Issue Brief: Public Pension Plan Investment Return Assumptions* (April 2014). Historically, private sector multiemployer plans have often used assumed return assumptions of 7.5 percent or higher. Between 1995 and 2007, large multiemployer plans used an average assumed return, weighted by plan liabilities, of

7.57 percent. For the 2010 plan year, multiemployer plans used an average assumed return, weighted by plan liabilities, of 7.52 percent. See Department of Labor, Department of the Treasury, and Pension Benefit Guaranty Corporation, *Multiemployer Pension Plans: Report to Congress Required by the Pension Protection Act of 2006* (Washington, D.C.: Jan. 22, 2013).

[149] An expert noted that Canadian public sector pensions are usually indexed to increases for inflation, and that while they typically use lower nominal assumed returns than US plans, their inflation assumptions are also often lower (about 2 percent to 2.5 percent, where U.S. plans might more typically use 3 percent), and speculated that their salary growth assumptions are likely lower as well. The expert said that the resulting Canadian funding target still ends up being more conservative (i.e., higher) than in the U.S., but the difference is not as great as the difference in valuation discount rates would suggest.

[150] As of December 2013, the maximum rate was set at 4.2 percent. See appendix IV for more details.

[151] The regulator also pointed out that, as most pension liabilities in the U.K. are in some way linked to inflation, this rate is about 1.1 percent higher than the index-linked government bond yield.

[152] The average excess returns are based on valuations for plans in recovery, submitted between September 2011 and September 2012 to the Pensions Regulator. As discussed earlier, plans in recovery are allowed to assume higher returns, over the recovery phase, than the discount rate used to calculate plan liabilities, provided that the recovery plan return assumption is justified by the investment strategy.

[153] As discussed, for financial reporting purposes, private sector plan sponsors in Canada, the Netherlands, and the United Kingdom often follow the accounting standards promulgated by IASB. U.K. plan sponsors will often follow the local U.K. accounting standards promulgated by FRC (the standards are referred to as Financial Reporting Standards) or the IASB standards.

[154] Each country's retirement system reflects that country's unique historical and political experience, making generalizations difficult. For example, the Netherland's adherence to market-interest valuation principles using strict risk-based solvency requirements may in part reflect the absence of a pension insurance system. Or, in the United Kingdom, the discretion plan sponsors have in determining their discount rate and approach under the Scheme Specific Funding framework may reflect the U.K.'s prior experience under a more rules-based regulatory regime.

[155] For financial reporting purposes, the discount rate will switch to a blended approach once new GASB standards are fully in effect, but industry experts have indicated that in most cases the resulting discount rate is likely to be closer to the assumed-return approach.

[156] As discussed, the FASB bond-based discount rate referenced here refers to requirements for plan sponsor, and not individual plan, financial reporting.

[157] In the United States, funding discount rates for private sector single-employer plans are fixed in law and Treasury performs the necessary data gathering and calculations to arrive at these rates. Private sector multiemployer and public plans have greater discretion in setting their discount rate.

[158] Actuarial reports are prepared by the plan actuary and are typically submitted on a tri- annual basis to the regulating entity, except for federally registered plans and for plans registered with the Quebec regulator, where actuarial reports are generally submitted on an annual basis. Plans that fall below certain funding levels may also be required to file on an annual basis.

[159] For example, OSFI officials told us that a funding discount rate not to exceed 6.25 percent applies to all federally-regulated pension plans registered under Canada's Pension Benefits Standards Act of 1985. This was reduced from 6.5 percent effective April 2013. These plans include primarily private sector plans, but also include some pension plans provided by certain public sector employers.

[160] For example, one expert indicated that a current best-estimate assumed return in Canada might be about 7 or 7.2 percent, but that subtracting a margin for adverse deviation might bring the assumption down to 6 percent. However, another expert told us that it is often difficult to tell if a plan is using a margin for adverse deviation, that any margin matters less than the actuary's expectation of future returns, that most plans probably do not use a margin, and that what ultimately matters is the net assumption used.

[161] Discounting guidelines and practices for federal pension plans are outside of the scope of this report. Information on PBGC's discount rate practices was provided as background.

[162] Multiemployer plans have a choice of actuarial cost methods under ERISA for determining the accrued liability on which minimum required contributions are primarily based. Multiemployer plans also disclose, on Schedule MB of Form 5500, two liability measures based on the unit credit actuarial cost method: an accrued liability using the plan's assumed return discount rate, and a measure called the current liability using a discount rate based on a 4-year weighted average of 30-year Treasury rates.

[163] More precisely, for pension benefit formulas based on future compensation, such as final-pay and career-average-pay pension formulas, the FASB method of attributing benefits to years of service is the same as the projected unit credit actuarial cost method. For flat benefit formulas (i.e., formulas that are not based on pay), a projection of future pay increases is irrelevant and unnecessary.

[164] Under ERISA, while plan sponsors may elect from two options (whether to use historically averaged rates or more current market rates), within each option the specific rates are defined by law and published by Treasury.

[165] FASB standards require discount rates to reflect the rate at which pension benefits could be effectively settled. In estimating these "settlement rates," plan sponsors have discretion in interpreting and applying this requirement. They can look either at available information about rates implicit in the pricing of current annuity contracts or rates of return on high-quality bonds that are currently and expected to be available that match the duration of the pension benefits; in practice, discount rates derived from high-quality bonds are typically used. Because current bond rates are observable in the market, there are fairly narrow limits to how much a FASB discount rate can vary and still be considered reasonable. Jon Waite, *Pension Accounting Research Series. 2013: An Update for Disclosures for 2012* (SEI Institutional Group, 2012).

[166] For private sector single-employer plan sponsors who elect to use historically averaged rates, under a simplified three-segment yield curve, the interest rates as prescribed by Treasury with respect to any month, prior to the MAP-21 adjustments, reflect the average, for the 24 month period ending with the month preceding such month, of monthly yields on investment grade corporate bonds with varying maturities and that are in the top 3 quality levels available (i.e., AAA, AA, and A). For private sector single-employer plan sponsors who elect to use more current market interest rates without historical averaging, the interest rates prescribed by Treasury, using a full yield curve approach, are determined in the same way as the rates used for the segment rate approach but without 24-month averaging. The market interest rates for any month, prior to any historical averaging, are based on an average of daily rates over the course of the month. Further, plan sponsors can elect to use rates as of an "applicable month," consistently applied from year to year, which can be the month containing the plan's annual valuation date or any of the preceding four months.

[167] Legislation was enacted in August 2014 that further extends the use of 25-year averaging of interest rates for determining minimum funding standards for private sector single-employer plans. Pub. L. No. 113-159, 128 Stat. 1839.

[168] Jon Waite, *Pension Accounting Research Series. 2013: An Update for Disclosures for2012* (SEI Institutional Group, 2012).

[169] Some bond-based approaches smooth interest rates by averaging previous years' interest rates to arrive at a discount rate, but equity returns would still not be relevant.

[170] Other experts argue that, on the contrary, investment risk in risky assets such as equities increases in magnitude the longer the time horizon.

[171] 2013 data was not yet available when we performed our analyses.

[172] They contain three independent 29-year data points, from 1926-1954, 1955-1983, and 1984-2012.

[173] For example, the years 1955-1983 are in 30 of the 58 rolling 30-year periods, while the years 1926 and 2012 are each in only one of the 58 periods.

[174] Unless otherwise noted, the returns in this section are all geometric means rather than arithmetic means. See discussion at end of this section.

[175] This is a simplified "arithmetic" example, ignoring the effects of compounding.

[176] Over time, a growing plan will add new members and generally contribute increasing amounts of money compared to the payments it makes to beneficiaries. On the other hand, a maturing plan will begin to deplete its assets as it makes increasingly higher benefit payments against its contribution base.

[177] See appendix I for more detail on our assumptions.

[178] Period 1 is from 1926 to 1954; period 2 is from 1955 to 1983; period 3 is from 1984 to 2012.

[179] As previously reported, since 2008, the combination of fiscal pressures and increasing contribution requirements has spurred many states and localities to take action to strengthen the financial condition of their plans for the long-term, often packaging multiple changes together, such as reducing benefits, increasing member contributions, and switching to a hybrid approach. We found that 35 states have reduced pension benefits, mostly for future employees due to legal provisions protecting benefits for current employees and retirees. A few states, like Colorado, have reduced postretirement benefit increases for all members and beneficiaries of their pension plans. See GAO

[180] The only exception is if every annual return is the same, in which case, the geometric and arithmetic means will be equal.

[181] Employees" refers to employees in the public and private sector and includes self-employed workers in incorporated business (with and without paid help). Registered pension plans are plans established by either employers or unions to provide retirement income to employees. Statistics Canada, Pension Plans in Canada and Labour Force Survey (2011).

[182] A margin for adverse deviation is a provision that can be applied to an actuarial assumption in a manner that produces higher cost, or lower revenue, than a best-estimate assumption in order to provide a margin of safety against the risk that actual experience proves to be less favorable than the best-estimate assumption. For example, if the best-estimate of future investment returns is 7 percent and a margin for adverse deviation of 0.5 percent is applied, then the assumed return net of the margin would be 6.5 percent.

[183] One exception is the province of Prince Edward Island, which does not have a pensions regulatory body.

[184] An exception is Quebec, which one expert told us has many differences in pension regulation compared to the rest of Canada.

[185] In this report, the Netherlands' use of the Euro swap curve to discount pension liabilities is also referred to as a bond-based approach.

[186] A forward rate is a rate of interest for a future period that would equate the total return of a long-term bond with that of a strategy of rolling over shorter-term bonds. The forward rate is inferred from a yield curve.

[187] In 2008, the recovery period for plans under the base funding threshold was extended by the government from 3 to 5 years as a vast majority of plans had to file recovery plans. As of July 2013, the regulator told us that there are still 70 plans in recovery status in this, the fifth year. In response, the regulator is in the process of contemplating more comprehensive changes to the pension regulatory system.

[188] For example, using maximum return assumptions of 7 percent for equities and 4.2 percent for bonds (the current predetermined maximum bond-based discount rate as introduced by the DNB), a static portfolio allocation of 60 percent in equities and 40 percent in bonds would

result in a composite assumed return of about 5.9 percent. The actual composite assumed return could be even lower since the portfolio may contain shorter duration bonds which would likely yield less than 4.2 percent under current conditions.

189 Workplace pension plans include defined benefit, defined contribution, and other types of pension plans.

190 The regulation states that "the rates of interest used to discount future payments of benefits must be chosen prudently, taking into account either or both–(i) the yield on assets held by the scheme to fund future benefits and the anticipated future investment returns, and (ii) the market redemption yields on government or other high-quality bonds."

191 Accounting standards developed by the FRC are contained in Financial Reporting Standards, referred to as FRS.

In: Pension Plan Valuation
Editor: Patricia Edwards
ISBN: 978-1-63483-238-0

Chapter 2

MULTIEMPLOYER DEFINED BENEFIT (DB) PENSION PLANS: A PRIMER AND ANALYSIS OF POLICY OPTIONS*

John J. Topoleski

SUMMARY

Multiemployer defined benefit (DB) pension plans are pensions sponsored by more than one employer and maintained as part of a collective bargaining agreement. About 3.2% of all DB pension plans, covering 25% of all DB pension plan participants, are multiemployer plans. Nearly all of the remaining DB pension plans are maintained by a single employer. A few DB pension plans are maintained by more than one employer but are not maintained under a collective bargaining agreement. In DB pension plans, participants receive a monthly benefit in retirement that is based on a formula. In multiemployer DB pensions, the formula typically multiplies a dollar amount by the number of years of service the employee has worked for employers that participate in the DB plan.

DB pension plans are subject to funding rules in the Internal Revenue Code (26 U.S.C. §431) to ensure they have sufficient resources from which to pay promised benefits. Because single employer and

---

* This is an edited, reformatted and augmented version of a Congressional Research Service publication R43305, prepared for Members and Committees of Congress dated October 7, 2014.

multiemployer DB pension plans have different structures, Congress has established separate funding rules for these plans. The funding rules for multiemployer DB pension plans are set to expire at the end of 2014, and Congress has been considering proposals that would alter these rules.

Although most multiemployer DB pension plans have sufficient resources from which to pay their promised benefits, a few large plans are expected to become insolvent in the next 20 years. The Pension Benefit Guaranty Corporation (PBGC) is a U.S. government agency that insures the benefits of participants in private-sector DB pension plans. As with the funding rules, Congress established separate PBGC programs to insure single and multiemployer DB pensions. For example, PBGC becomes the trustee of terminated single employer DB pension plans. PBGC does not become the trustee of multiemployer DB pension plans; rather, it makes loans to insolvent multiemployer DB plans so the plans may continue to pay participants' guaranteed benefits.

Although PBGC has sufficient resources to make loans to smaller multiemployer DB plans, the insolvency of a large multiemployer DB pension plan would likely result in a substantial strain on PBGC's multiemployer insurance program. In the absence of increased financial resources for PBGC, participants in insolvent multiemployer DB pension plans might not receive all of the benefits guaranteed by PBGC. In a report released in June 2014, PBGC indicated that the multiemployer insurance program is highly likely to become insolvent by 2025.

INTRODUCTION

A pension is a voluntary benefit offered by employers to assist employees in providing for their financial security in retirement. Department of Labor (DOL) data in 2013 indicated that 65% of full-time workers in the United States participated in a retirement plan sponsored by their employer.[1] The two types of pension plans are defined contribution (DC) plans (of which the 401(k) plan is the most common), in which participants have individual accounts that are the basis of income in retirement; and defined benefit (DB) plans, in which participants receive regular monthly benefit payments in retirement (which some refer to as a "traditional" type of pension).[2] Pension plans are also classified by whether they are sponsored by one employer (single employer plans) or by more than one employer (multiemployer and multiple employer plans). Multiemployer pension plans are sponsored by employers in the same industry and maintained as part of a collective bargaining agreement. Multiple employer plans are sponsored by more than one employer but are not maintained as part of a collective bargaining agreement. Multiple employer pension plans are not common.[3]

Nearly all private-sector pension plans are governed by the Employee Retirement Income Security Act of 1974 (ERISA; P.L. 93-406), which is enforced by the Department of the Treasury, the DOL, and the Pension Benefit Guaranty Corporation (PBGC).[4] Because of differences in the structure of the plans, single and multiemployer DB pension plans have different rules under some sections of ERISA. Examples include the existence of separate funding rules for each type of plan and pension insurance program.

Multiemployer DB plans are of current concern to Congress for several reasons:

- the funding rules for these plans expire at the end of 2014, so Congress must decide whether, and in which ways, to alter the funding rules;
- some plans have insufficient plan assets from which to pay 100% of the benefits promised to plan participants;
- a few very large multiemployer DB pension plans are in such poor financial condition that they are expected to become insolvent within 10 years or 20 years; and
- because the liabilities of these large pension plans are so great, PBGC would likely be unable to continue to guarantee participants' benefits if one or two of these plans became insolvent.

Possible solutions to plan underfunding could involve some combination of increased contributions from the employers that sponsor pension plans, cuts in future benefits to plan participants who are currently working, cuts in current benefits to retired participants, or financial assistance from the U.S. government.

Background on Pensions

To protect the interests of pension plan participants and beneficiaries, Congress enacted ERISA (P.L. 93-406). ERISA is codified in the U.S. Code in Title 26 (Internal Revenue Code, or IRC) and Title 29 (Labor Code) and sets standards that pension plans must follow with regard to plan participation (who must be covered); minimum vesting requirements (how long a person must work for an employer to be covered); plan funding (how much must be set aside to pay for future benefits); and fiduciary duties, which require that a pension plan be operated in the sole interests of plan participants by plan sponsors, administrators, and others who oversee the plan. ERISA established PBGC, which is an independent federal agency that insures DB pension plans covered by ERISA. ERISA covers only private-sector pension plans and exempts pension plans established by the federal, state, and local governments and by churches.

Pension plans may be classified in a variety of ways, such as whether they receive tax preferences, whether they are sponsored by one or more than one employer, and whether the benefits are payable as a lifetime annuity at retirement or accrue in accounts for each of the participants.

Tax-Qualified Pension Plans

Sponsors of pension plans may choose for their plans to be tax qualified. Tax-qualified plans receive certain tax advantages. For example, employer contributions to qualified DB plans are tax-deductible expenses for employers in the year contributions are made. Qualified plans also meet IRC requirements with respect to vesting schedules (which determine when participants have a legal right to their benefits) and funding requirements (which determine the amounts plan sponsors must contribute to the plans they sponsor). Generally, qualified DB pension plans must pre-fund future benefits.[5] Non-qualified pension plans are not required by the IRC to be pre-funded. Because one of the requirements to be a tax-qualified plan is to cover a broad range of employees in a company, non-qualified pension plans are designed for top-level executives and other highly compensated employees.

Single Employer, Multiple Employer, and Multiemployer Pension Plans

Pension plans are also classified by whether they are sponsored by one employer (single employer pension plans) or by more than one employer (multiple and multiemployer pension plans). Most pension plans are sponsored by one employer. DOL data indicate that 99.6% of all pension plans (covering 91.4% of all pension plan participants) are single employer pension plans.[6]

Single Employer Pension Plans

Single employer pension plans are sponsored by one employer and cover eligible workers employed by the plan sponsor. When an employee stops working for the employer sponsoring the plan, the worker stops accruing benefits under that plan. The sponsor may decide to cease offering its employees benefits under the plan, in which case the plan may be frozen or terminated. If a DB pension plan is frozen, participants no longer accrue benefits but employers maintain responsibility for the frozen plan (for example, employers may have to make additional contributions to make up for funding shortfalls that may result from decreases in the value of plan assets). Alternatively, employers may decide to terminate their pension plans. Employers that terminate their DB pension plans must guarantee participants' future benefits by purchasing annuities (a guaranteed monthly payment) from an insurance company for each participant's accrued benefit. If underfunded DB pension plans are terminated pursuant to company bankruptcy, PBGC becomes the trustee of the plans and pays participants their promised benefits, up to a statutory maximum benefit.[7]

Multiple Employer Pension Plans

Multiple employer pension plans are sponsored by more than one employer and are not maintained under collective bargaining agreements. They are treated as single employer pension plans for the purposes of funding rules.

Multiemployer Pension Plans

Multiemployer pension plans are sponsored by more than one employer and are maintained under collective bargaining agreements. Participants continue to accrue benefits while working for any employer that participates in the plan. Multiemployer pension plans pool risk so that the withdrawal of a few employers from the plan does not place the plan in financial jeopardy. However, in recent years, an increasing number of employers have left multiemployer pension plans (either voluntarily or through employer bankruptcy). As a result of declines in the value of plan assets (such as occurred during the 2008 financial market decline, some participants who worked for employers that withdrew from the plan may have unfunded vested benefits in the plan.

DB and DC Plans

Pension plans are either DB or DC. Over the past 30 years, employers have been offering fewer DB plans and more DC pensions. DOL data indicate that 64.2% of all pension plan participants were in DB plans in 1981, and that percentage declined to 31.5% in 2011.[8]

DB Pension Plans

Participants in DB pension plans receive monthly payments in retirement. In multiemployer DB pension plans, the payment is typically calculated as the length of service with employers that contribute to the plan multiplied by a dollar amount.[9] The payments are paid by the plan for the lifetime of the worker after he or she retires. Plan participants who are married may receive a joint-and-survivor annuity, which is an annuity payable for the lifetime of the participant or the participant's spouse, whichever is longer.

DB pension plans are generally funded entirely by employer contributions. DOL data in 2011 indicated that among private-sector workers who participated in DB plans, 4% were required to make an employee contribution to the plans. Among public-sector workers who participated in DB plans, 79% were required to make a contribution to their DB pension plans.[10]

DC Pension Plans

Workers in DC pension plans contribute a percentage of their wages to an individually established account. Employers may also contribute a match to the DC plan, which is an additional contribution equal to some or all of the worker's contribution. The account accrues investment returns and is then used as a basis for income in retirement. DC plans do not provide guarantees of lifetime income, unless participants purchase an annuity. Examples of DC plans are 401(k), 403(b), and 4057(b) plans and the Thrift Savings Plan (TSP).[11]

Data on Pension Plans and Participants

Table 1 provides information on the number of single and multiemployer DC and DB pension plans in 2011 (the most recent year for which data is available) and the number of active and retired participants by plan type. In 2011, there were 1,442 multiemployer DB pension plans that covered 10.4 million participants, of which 40.1% were active participants, meaning that 59.9% were retired (thus receiving benefits). DB pension plans that have high percentages of active workers are better able to rely on future contributions from plan sponsors to make up for plan underfunding. This is because, *on a per participant basis*, employers' contributions toward the underfunding will be lower in plans with higher percentages of active workers.

Table 1. Single and Multiemployer Pension Plans in 2011

	Single Employer Pension Plans		Multiemployer Pension Plans	
	Defined Contribution	Defined Benefit	Defined Contribution	Defined Benefit
Number of Plans	637,086	43,813	1,299	1,442
Number of Active Participants (millions)	70.3	12.3	3.4	4.2
Number of Retired Participants (millions)	14.0	18.1	1.1	6.3
Total Participants (millions)	84.3	30.4	4.4	10.4
Active as a Percentage of Total Participants	83.4%	40.5%	76.3%	40.1%
Plan Assets (billions)	$3,657.7	$2,050.6	$171.8	$465.5

Source: Department of Labor (DOL), Employee Benefits Security Administration, Private Pension Plan Bulletin Abstract of 2011 Form 5500 Annual Reports.

Notes: Multiple employer pension plans are categorized as single employer pension plans on Form 5500. Active participants include any workers currently in employment covered by a plan and who are earning or retaining credited service under a plan. This category includes any non-vested former employees who have not yet incurred a break in service. Active participants also include individuals who are eligible to elect to have the employer make payments to a 401(k) plan.

Funding Levels in Multiemployer DB Pension Plans

The funding levels of multiemployer DB pension plans are varied: some plans are well funded and have adequate funds from which to pay all of their promised benefits, and a few plans are poorly funded and may become insolvent within 10 years to 20 years. An insolvent multiemployer DB pension plan has depleted all of its assets and is unable to pay all of its current benefit obligations. Insolvent DB pension plans are eligible to receive financial assistance from PBGC. The Pension Protection Act of 2006 (PPA; P.L. 109-280) requires a plan that has a funding shortfall below specified levels to notify DOL of the plan's funding status and establish a plan to improve funding levels over time.

Background on Multiemployer DB Plan Funding

DB pension benefits are accrued by eligible employees while working. The benefit is paid, typically as a monthly annuity, during the worker's retirement. The benefits in DB plans subject to ERISA are required to be pre-funded, which means that in the current year the plan sponsor sets aside adequate funds, taking into account expected future investment returns, for pension benefits earned in that year.[12] Plan sponsors may also be required to make additional contributions for investment losses that occurred in previous years and increases in the present value of future plan obligations. Plan participants receive their monthly benefit in retirement from these funds that have been set aside.

The required contributions for employers in multiemployer DB pension plans are fixed for several years as established in collective bargaining agreements. Various situations have led to many pension plans having a smaller amount of funds than the amount of benefits that have been promised by the plan. These situations include declines in the values of plan assets (such as occurred during the stock market decline in 2008) and increases in the current value of future benefits (such as occurred when interest rates declined as a result of the Federal Reserve's efforts to strengthen the economy). The *Appendix* provides background for understanding pension plan funding issues.

Funding Standard Accounts and Funding Deficiencies

Multiemployer DB plans maintain funding standard accounts, which facilitate the administration of funding requirements. Charges (debits) to the account reduce the account balance and include the cost of benefits earned by participants during the year and investment losses.[13] Credits increase the funding standard account and include employer contributions to the plan and investment gains.[14]

When the total credits to a multiemployer DB pension plan exceed the total charges, the plan has a "credit balance" and no contributions are required until future charges eliminate the credit balance. When the total charges exceed the total credits, a funding deficiency results and additional contributions to the plan may be required. According the PBGC, 90 plans (out of 1,471 plans) reported funding deficiencies in 2010.[15]

Of these 90 plans,

- three plans, each with more than 10,000 participants, had individual funding deficiencies of between $35 million and $99 million;

- one plan with between 5,000 and 10,000 participants had a funding deficiency more than $100 million; and
- two plans, each with more than 10,000 participants, had individual funding deficiencies of more than $100 million.

Withdrawal Liability

When a company wishes to exit a multiemployer DB plan, the company is responsible for its withdrawal liability, defined as its share of unfunded vested benefits (benefits to which participants have a contractual right but which the plan has insufficient assets to pay).[16] In instances in which an employer withdraws from a multiemployer DB pension plan because of the employer's bankruptcy, it may not be possible to recover the employer's withdrawal liability. As a result, there may be plan participants with vested benefits who worked for an employer that no longer participates in the plan. These participants are sometimes called *orphan participants* because they do not have an employer that will make additional contributions to the plan for their unfunded benefits. The existence of orphan plan participants can result in a worsening funding situation for the multiemployer plan, because DB plan assets are comingled in a trust and are not assigned to a particular employer's contributions or participant's benefit. Thus, benefit payments for all participants draw down general plan assets.[17]

Reporting of Plan Funded Status

PPA requires that the actuary of a multiemployer DB pension plan annually certify the plan's status in one of three categories based on, among other factors, the funded status of the plan.[18] A plan can be in critical status, endangered status, or neither category. A plan in critical or endangered status must take measures to improve its financial conditions.

Critical (Red Zone) Status

A plan is in *critical status* if any of the following conditions apply: (1) the plan's funding ratio is less than 65% and in the next six years the value of the plan's assets and contributions will be less than the value of benefits; (2) in the current year, the plan is not expected to receive 100% of the contributions required by the plan sponsor, or the plan is not expected to receive 100% of the required contributions for any of the next three years (four years if the plan's funding percentage is 65% or less); (3) the plan is expected to be insolvent within five years (within seven years if the plan's funding percentage is 65% or less); or (4) the cost of the current year's benefits and the interest on unfunded liabilities are greater than the contributions for the current year, the present value of benefits for inactive participants is greater than the present value of benefits for active participants, and there is expected to be a funding deficiency within five years.

Plans in critical status must adopt a rehabilitation plan. The rehabilitation plan is a range of options (such as increased employer contributions and reductions in future benefits accruals) that, when adopted, will allow the plan to emerge from critical status during a 10-year *rehabilitation period*. If a plan cannot emerge from critical status by the end of the rehabilitation period using reasonable measures, it must either install measures to emerge from critical status at a later time (after the end of the rehabilitation period) or forestall insolvency. Plans in critical status may not increase benefits during the rehabilitation period.

Plans in critical status must provide notice to plan participants, beneficiaries, the collective bargaining parties, PBGC, and DOL.[19]

Endangered (Yellow Zone) Status

A plan is in *endangered status* if (1) the plan's funding ratio is less than 80% funded or (2) the plan has a funding deficiency in the current year or is projected to have one in the next six years. A plan is seriously endangered if it meets both of these criteria.

Plans in endangered status must adopt a funding improvement plan, which is a range of options (such as increased contributions and reductions in future benefit accruals) that, when adopted, will reduce the plan's underfunding by 33% during a 10-year *funding improvement period*. Plans in seriously endangered status must adopt a funding improvement plan that will reduce underfunding by 20% during a 15-year funding improvement period. Plans in endangered or seriously endangered status cannot increase benefits during the funding improvement period.

Plans in endangered status must provide notice to plan participants, beneficiaries, the collective bargaining parties, PBGC, and DOL.[20]

Green Status

Plans that are neither in critical or endangered status are considered to be in *green status*. These plans most likely will be able to pay all of the participants' benefits without changes to employers' contributions or participants' benefits.

Table 2 provides the number of multiemployer DB plan certifications within each funded status category for the 1,312 plans that reported their plan certification in 2011.[21]

Table 2. Defined Benefit Multiemployer Plan Certification in 2011

Status	Number of Plans	
Neither Critical nor Endangered (Green Zone)	780	(59.5%)
Endangered (Yellow Zone)	196	(14.9%)
Seriously Endangered	17	(1.3%)
Critical (Red Zone)	319	(24.3%)

Source: Pension Benefit Guaranty Corporation (PBGC), Multiemployer Pension Plans: Report to Congress Required by the Pension Protection Act of 2006, January 22, 2013, p. 40, http://www.pbgc.gov/documents/pbgc-reportmultiemployer-pension-plans.pdf.

PBGC Multiemployer Insurance Program

PBGC is a federal government agency created by ERISA in 1974 to protect the benefits of participants in private-sector DB pension plans. PBGC operates two insurance programs: a single employer insurance program and a multiemployer insurance program. The two programs function quite differently. In the single employer program, PBGC becomes the trustee of terminated, underfunded DB pension plans and pays benefits up to a statutory maximum amount. In the case of multiemployer plans, PBGC does not insure against termination. Rather, when a multiemployer DB pension plan becomes insolvent and is unable to pay participants their promised benefits, PBGC provides financial assistance in the form of loans (which are not expected to be repaid) made to multiemployer DB plans. As a condition for the loans, plans must reduce participants' benefits to a statutory maximum benefit.

PBGC's multiemployer insurance program receives revenues from two sources: (1) premium revenue paid by the sponsors of multiemployer pension plans and (2) interest income from holdings of U.S. Treasury debt. Premium revenue is placed in a revolving fund that, by law, is invested in U.S. Treasury debt.

In its FY2012 report on its expected financial operations in the future, PBGC indicated that there was a 36% probability the multiemployer insurance program would become insolvent by 2022 and a 91% probability that it would become insolvent by 2032.

The September 30, 2013, financial statements of PBGC indicated the following for FY2013:[22]

- The multiemployer program had assets of $1.7 billion, nearly all of which was invested in U.S. Treasury securities.[23]
- Total liabilities were $10.0 billion, nearly all of which was the present value of the financial assistance to currently insolvent and probably insolvent plans.[24]
- Premium income in FY2013 was $110 million.
- Investment losses in FY2013 were $96 million.
- Loans to insolvent plans totaled $89 million in FY2013.
- The deficit (assets minus liabilities) in the multiemployer program was $8.3 billion, an increase of $3.0 billion from FY2012.

Current and Future Financial Assistance to Multiemployer Pension Plans

PBGC provides financial assistance to insolvent multiemployer pension plans. In addition to providing details about the number of plans receiving financial assistance, PBGC estimates the number of plans that might need financial assistance in the future. Potential future financial assistance is categorized as either (1) probable or (2) reasonably possible, depending on whether the PBGC expects to provide the assistance (1) within 10 years or (2) between 10 years and 20 years.

Plans Currently Receiving Financial Assistance

Forty-four multiemployer plans received financial assistance in FY2013 that totaled $89 million. The net liability associated with these plans was $1.4 billion.[25]

Probable Exposure to Future Financial Assistance

Plans are classified as probable if the plan is (1) terminated and underfunded but not yet receiving financial assistance or (2) ongoing but expected to be insolvent within 10 years. In FY2013,

- 65 multiemployer plans had been terminated but had not yet started receiving financial assistance. The net liability associated with these plans was $1.9 billion.
- 64 plans were ongoing but expected to be insolvent within 10 years. The net liability associated with these plans was $6.7 billion.

Reasonably Possible Exposure to Future Financial Assistance

Plans are classified as reasonably possible exposure to future financial assistance if the plan is ongoing but is projected to be insolvent in 10 years to 20 years. Approximately $26 billion of the $36.7 billion in reasonably possible future financial assistance is a result of the potential insolvency of two large plans. One plan, classified by PBGC in the "transportation, communications, and utilities" industry, had a net liability of $20 billion as of the end of FY2013.[26] A second plan, classified by PBGC in the "agriculture, mining, and construction" industry, had a net liability of $6 billion at the end of FY2013.[27]

PBGC Guarantees

PBGC guarantees benefits in pension plans up to a statutory maximum level. When an insolvent multiemployer DB pension plan becomes insolvent, the plan must reduce participants' benefit to the PBGC maximum amount before the plan receives the assistance. The statutory annual maximum benefit in multiemployer plans that receive financial assistance from PBGC is the product of a participant's years of service multiplied by the sum of (1) 100% of the first $11 of the monthly benefit accrual rate and (2) 75% of the next $33 of the accrual rate. For a participant with 30 years of service, the statutory annual maximum benefit is $12,870 in 2014.[28]

PBGC Premium and Investment Income in FY2013

PBGC reported $110 million in premium income from multiemployer plans in FY2013. PBGC also reported $96 million in investment losses from holdings of U.S. Treasury debt. Premiums are placed in a revolving fund, which, by law, must be invested in Treasury securities.

PBGC Premium Levels

The PBGC multiemployer insurance program is funded by a per participant premium paid by each pension plan. In 2014, the sponsors of multiemployer DB pension plans pay an annual premium of $12 for each participant in the plan. Section 40222 of the Moving Ahead for Progress in the 21st Century Act (MAP-21; P.L. 112-141) increased the premium from $9 per participant to $12 per participant. MAP-21 also required that the premium be indexed to inflation beginning in 2014.

Inadequacy of PBGC Premiums

Unlike the single employer insurance program, PBGC does not become trustee of insolvent multiemployer pension plans. For this reason, the only sources of funding for the financial assistance to insolvent multiemployer pension plans are (1) the collection of premiums that multiemployer plan sponsors pay to PBGC and (2) interest income from the investment of past premium income in U.S. Treasury bonds. If the amount of financial assistance were to exceed the amount of premium revenue, then the revolving fund containing the investments in U.S. Treasuries could become depleted.

As mentioned above, PBGC estimated its *probable exposure* to future financial assistance to be $8.6 billion[29] over the next 10 years and its *reasonably possible exposure* to future financial assistance to be $36.7 billion. The premium income in PBGC's multiemployer program was $110 million in FY2012. PBGC has indicated that the multiemployer insurance program is likely to become insolvent in 10 years to 15 years, even before any new financial obligations are added.[30]

Premium levels are likely inadequate to provide continued financial assistance to insolvent multiemployer plans and could exhaust PBGC's ability to guarantee participants' benefits. PBGC has indicated that once resources are exhausted in its multiemployer program, insolvent plans would be required to reduce benefits to levels that could be sustained through premium collections only. PBGC premiums are set by law. Many stakeholders, such as Members of Congress and plan sponsors, might be reluctant to raise premiums to the levels necessary to fund promised benefits if the scenario in the *reasonably possible exposure* developed.

MULTIEMPLOYER DB PENSION PLAN POLICY ISSUES

Policy makers have been giving increased attention to issues concerning multiemployer DB pension plans and PBGC's multiemployer insurance program.[31] One reason is that because the funding rules for multiemployer DB pension plans sunset on December 31, 2014, some Members of Congress have expressed a desire to address the challenges faced by the sponsors of multiemployer DB pension plans and by PBGC's multiemployer insurance program.[32]

Likely Insolvency of a Few Large Multiemployer Pension Plans and PBGC Insurance Program

Although many multiemployer DB pension plans are underfunded, most can expect their funding position to improve with modest changes to the plan, such as increased employer contributions. However, a few large multiemployer plans are in very poor financial condition and are likely to become insolvent.

Insolvent DB multiemployer pension plans are eligible for financial assistance from PBGC. PBGC has sufficient assets from which to provide financial assistance to currently insolvent plans and to smaller multiemployer plans that may become insolvent in the future. However, if one or more large multiemployer plans become insolvent, PBGC would likely have insufficient resources from which to pay 100% of the benefits owed to plan participants.

PBGC has indicated that once it has exhausted the assets in the multiemployer insurance program revolving funds, it would be able to pay total benefits equal to total premium income. This would likely mean that participants' benefits would be cut to levels below the current maximum benefit.[33] In this scenario, if Congress wished to pay 100% of the participants' benefits, then premiums would have to rise to levels that many plan sponsors, plan participants, and policy makers would find unreasonable.[34]

In its *FY2013 Projections Report* released on June 30, 2014, PBGC indicated that the multiemployer program is more likely than not to become insolvent within 8 years, highly likely to become insolvent within 11 years, and facing a 99% likelihood of insolvency within 20 years.[35]

The estimates presented in the projections report suggest that PBGC's multiemployer insurance program will face significant financial challenges over the next 10 years. The value of assets in the multiemployer program at the end of FY2013 was $1.7 billion, and PBGC estimated the present value of the next 10 years of insurance premiums to be $1.2 billion. These two sources of funds total $2.9 billion and represent the amount of resources available to PBGC from which to provide future financial assistance over the next 10 years. PBGC estimated the present value of future financial assistance to multiemployer plans from FY2014 to FY2023 to be $6.1 billion. This deficit of $3.2 billion is the amount by which PBGC will be unable to provide sufficient financial assistance for plans to pay the PBGC guaranteed maximum benefit ($12,970 per year per participant) over this period. The projections report noted that plans will likely require significant amounts of financial assistance even after FY2024 because the present value of PBGC's financial position in 2023 was estimated to be a deficit of $50 billion.[36]

Proposals for Multiemployer DB Pension Reform

The National Coordinating Committee for Multiemployer Plans (NCCMP) is an organization that represents a number of multiemployer pension plans.[37] NCCMP created a Retirement Security Review Commission to gather input from a coalition of employers and labor groups for multiemployer DB pension reform proposals. In February 2013, the commission issued a report to advance a proposal that it indicated would reform and strengthen the multiemployer pension system.[38] The commission proposed the following: (1) reforms to existing funding rules for multiemployer pension plans; (2) solutions to address deeply troubled multiemployer DB pension plans (plans that are expected to become insolvent in the next 10 years); and (3) new plan designs to encourage the creation of new multiemployer plans.[39]

Recommendations for Changes to Existing Funding Rules

The commission's 13 recommendations for changes to the funding rules for multiemployer DB pensions would

- permit plans to enter critical status if they anticipate being in that status in the next five years. Under current law, multiemployer plans are required to make changes to the plan structure when they enter critical status. However, plans cannot make changes even if they anticipate entering that status (they must wait until they enter that status);

- allow plans that emerge from critical status to not reenter critical status for at least one year following their emergence. Under current law, because different criteria exist in the funding status tests for plans emerging from critical status, some plans emerge from and then immediately reenter critical status;
- authorize plans that meet the criteria for endangered status but have funding improvement plans that do not require additional contributions or benefit changes to not be certified as in endangered status. Some plans that enter endangered status do not have to make any changes to contributions or benefit levels to emerge from that status. Under current law, these plans continue to be classified as being in endangered status;
- permit plan actuaries for plans in endangered status, when developing funding improvement plans, to use the funding status as of the date of certification of the status rather than having to calculate the plan's funding status as of the beginning of the funding improvement plan. Under current law, plan actuaries must calculate the funding status at date of certification of endangered status and make a projection of the funding status at the beginning of the funding improvement period;
- allow plans in endangered status to adopt some of the rules currently available only to plans in critical status, including contribution decreases and the waiver of excise taxes. Some plans that are in endangered status actively seek to be placed in critical status because a number of the restrictions placed on plans in endangered status are more onerous than those for plans in critical status;
- provide for automatic triggers for funding relief when dramatic decline occur in financial markets. Under current law, Congress must authorize changes in funding rules, which can result in a delay between the onset of financial difficulties for pension plans and the implementation of funding relief;
- enable funding improvement plans and rehabilitation plans to specify the course of action if the collective bargaining agreement expires and the parties cannot agree on a schedule. Current law provides no guidance as to the course of action a plan must take if a collective bargaining agreement expires when a plan is in endangered or critical status;
- allow rules for plans in critical status to take priority over rules for plans in reorganization when both occur simultaneously. The

Multiemployer Pension Plan Amendments Act of 1980 (P.L. 96-364) required plans in weak financial condition to undergo reorganization and established rules for plans in reorganization to improve funding. There may be conflicts between some of the rules for plans that are both in reorganization and in endangered or critical status;

- permit contribution increases as part of a funding improvement plan or a rehabilitation plan to be disregarded in determining withdrawal liability. Plans that are in critical or endangered status could inadvertently make changes that could increase plans' withdrawal liability;
- provide pre-retirement survivor annuities to plan participants who die after the date of plan insolvency or termination. Plan participants in multiemployer plans that are insolvent or that have been terminated are currently ineligible for pre-retirement survivor annuities. This is in contrast to participants in single employer plans, who remain eligible for survivor annuities after plan termination;
- allow plans to pay certain additional benefits (a 13th check) that would not be considered a part of a participant's accrued benefit. Plans that experience favorable investment returns sometimes provide participants an additional benefit. If the 13th check is offered on a regular basis, then the benefit is considered a regular benefit, which cannot be reduced or eliminated;
- eliminate the potential exposure to an IRS excise tax for plans that were granted amortization extensions under PPA. Prior to PPA, in exchange for a schedule of funding improvements, the IRS allowed some plans to extend the length of time to make up for investment losses. As a result of the 2008 market downturn, many plans failed to meet the requirements for the schedule of funding improvements and are potentially subject to an IRS excise tax. PPA provided for amortization extensions that made the pre-PPA extensions unnecessary.
- permit plan participants to convert DC accounts into annuities payable from their DB pension plans. This would allow participants who have DC accounts to receive lifetime income from their DC plans.

In addition, the commission recommended changes to existing law that would ease multiemployer plan mergers and alliances and allow plans to harmonize the normal retirement age under the plan (generally age 65) to the age with the Social Security Retirement Age (age 67 for individuals born in 1960 and later).

Recommendations for Deeply Troubled Plans

Some multiemployer DB pension plans are in very poor financial condition and are likely to become insolvent. If one or two of the largest plans become insolvent, PBGC would likely have insufficient resources from which to guarantee participants' benefits. If PBGC is unable to pay participants' guaranteed benefits, it is unclear whether PBGC would receive financial assistance from the federal government. PBGC was established to be self-financing, and ERISA states that the "United States is not liable for any obligation or liability incurred by the corporation."[40] Some Members of Congress have expressed a reluctance to consider providing financial assistance to PBGC.[41]

Deeply troubled multiemployer DB plans have limited options to avoid insolvency. Increased contributions and cuts to adjustable benefits to active plan participants are likely to be insufficient to return these plans to solvency. Participants' benefits in insolvent plans would be reduced to the PBGC guaranteed levels, or possibly lower, if PBGC has insufficient resources from which to pay 100% of the benefits guaranteed to participants. The commission has proposed allowing plans that are projected to become insolvent within 20 years the ability to suspend benefit payments for both active participants and retirees. The commission proposes that the suspension of benefits would be equitable across active and retired participants and protect the most vulnerable segments of the population. Benefits would not be reduced to below 110% of the level guaranteed by PBGC.

Reducing retirees' benefits is likely to be a contentious issue.[42] For example, retirees may be asked to shoulder a burden that could otherwise be fixed by increased employer contributions. Another concern is that retirees, particularly the most vulnerable, might not have adequate representation in discussions of changes to deeply troubled multiemployer DB pensions.[43]

Proposals for New Plan Structures

The commission proposed two new structures for multiemployer DB pension plans: variable annuity plans and target benefit plans.

In the commission's proposal, a variable annuity pension plan would provide participants with a minimum benefit and would possibly provide additional benefits based on the investment performance of the plan's assets. Such a plan structure would mitigate, to some extent, employers' concerns about large and unexpected increases in contributions as a result of poor investment performance.

In the target benefit plan structure, employers would not have any withdrawal liability. Participants would bear the risk that the value of the plan's assets could decline, which could result in reduced benefits. To lessen the possibility of decline in the value of plan assets, the assets of target benefit plans would be invested in a conservative manner.[44]

APPENDIX. DEFINED BENEFIT PLAN FUNDING

This appendix provides background on basic concepts related to the funding of DB pension plans.

DB Plan Balance Sheet

Figure A-1 depicts a typical DB pension plan's balance sheet. It consists of plan assets, which are the value of the investments made with accrued employer (and employee, if any) contributions to the plan, and plan liabilities, which are the value of participants' benefits earned under the terms of the plan. Plan assets are invested in equities (such as publicly traded stock), debt (such as U.S. Treasury and corporate bonds), private equity, hedge funds, and real estate.

Assets	Liabilities
Investments (from contributions by plan sponsors)	Discounted Value of Future Benefit Payments

Source: Congressional Research Service (CRS).

Figure A-1. Typical Balance Sheet of a Defined Benefit Pension Plan.

DB Plan Funding Ratio

The funding ratio measures the adequacy of a DB pension plan's ability to pay for promised benefits. The funding ratio is calculated as

$$\frac{\text{Value of Plan Assets}}{\text{Present Value of Plan Liabilities}}$$

A funding ratio of 100% indicates that the DB plan has set aside enough funds, if the invested funds grow at the expected rate of return or better, to pay all of the plan's benefit obligations. Funding ratios that are less than 100% indicate that the DB plan will not be able to meet all of its future benefit obligations. Because benefit obligations are paid out over a period of 20 years to 30 years, participants in an underfunded plan will likely receive their promised benefits in the near term. However, if the underfunding persists without additional contributions, plan participants might not receive 100% of their promised benefits in the future.

In response to strong investment returns in the 1990s, many multiemployer DB pension plans increased benefits to participants. Many of these plans then became underfunded during the early 2000s as financial markets weakened. Their financial position worsened as a result of (1) stricter funding rules put in place in the Pension Protection Act of 2006 (P.L. 109-280), (2) the decline in equity markets in 2008, (3) low interest rates as a result of weak economic conditions, and (4) the bankruptcy of some of the firms participating in the plans.

The Value of Plan Assets

Pension plans report the value of plan assets using two methods: market values (the value at which each asset can be sold on a particular date) or smoothed values (the average of the past, and sometimes expected future, market values of each asset). The smoothing of asset values prevents large swings in asset values and creates a more predictable funding environment for plan sponsors. One of the drawbacks of smoothing is that smoothed asset values may be substantially different from market values. Some advocates of reporting market values note that smoothed values are often higher than market values (particularly during periods of market declines), which could overstate the financial health of some pension plans. Some advocates of smoothing argue that market values are useful only if a plan needs to know its liquidated value (e.g., if the plan had to pay all of its benefit obligations at one point in time), which is unlikely to be the case as most pension plans are likely to be ongoing concerns.

Plan Liabilities

A pension plan's benefits are a plan liability spread out over many years in the future. These future benefits are calculated and reported as current dollar values (also called present value). *Figure A-2* shows the process by which future benefits are discounted. Using a formula, benefits that are expected to be paid in a particular year in the future are calculated so they can be expressed as a current value. The process is called *discounting,* and it is the reverse of the process of *compounding*, which projects how much a dollar amount will be worth at a point in the future.

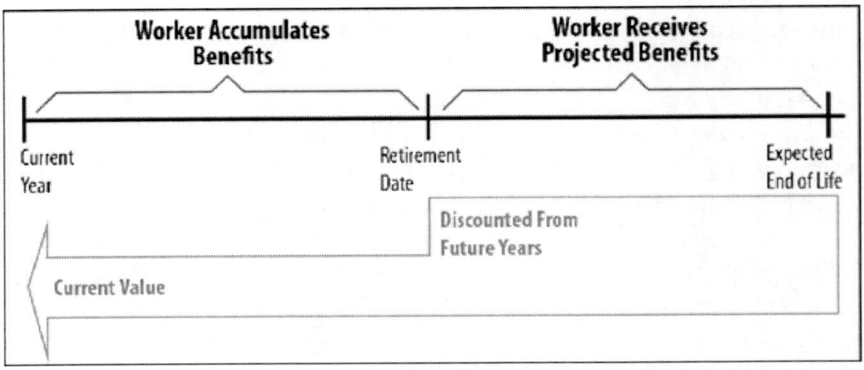

Source: CRS.

Figure A-2. How Future Pension Benefits Are Discounted.

$$\textbf{Current Value} = \frac{\textbf{Dollar Value of Future Benefit}}{\textbf{(Discount Rate)}^{\textbf{Number of Years in the Future}}}$$

Source: CRS.

Figure A-3. Present Value Formula.

For example, assuming a discount rate of 10%, \$121 in two years' time is worth $\frac{\$121}{(1.1)^2} = \$100$ today. The present value of a dollar amount is inversely related to both the discount rate and the number of years in the future. As the discount rate or number of years in the future increases, present value decreases; as the discount rate or number of years decreases, present value increases. In the above example, if the discount rate is 15%, then \$121 in two years' time is worth $\frac{\$121}{(1.15)^2} = \$91.49$ today, and \$121 in three years' time is worth $\frac{\$121}{(1.15)^3} = \$79.56.$

Discount Rate Used to Value Future Benefits

In the context of DB pension plans, plan actuaries calculate the present value of future benefit obligations by estimating (1) the dollar amount of the benefits accrued by plan participants and (2) the years in the future in which the benefits are expected to be paid. The Internal Revenue Code does not require multiemployer pension plans to use a specific discount rate to value their future benefit obligation. The assumptions a plan uses must be reasonable and offer the best estimate of the plan's expected experience.[45] In practice, multiemployer plans generally discount plan liabilities using the expected rate of return on the plan's assets. Since the economic downturn that began in 2008, the policy of the Federal Reserve has been to maintain low interest rates in an effort to stimulate the U.S. economy.[46] This sustained period of low interest rates is one of the factors that has contributed to worsening pension plan underfunding because low interest rates can lower the returns on stock, bonds, and other investments.[47]

Pension policy experts have several viewpoints on the appropriate discount rate that pension plans should use to value plan liabilities.[48] Broadly speaking, some actuaries recommend that pension plans discount future benefits using the expected rate of return on plan investments (the current practice for multiemployer DB pension plans). Some financial economists, by contrast, recommend that plans discount the liabilities using a discount rate that reflects the likelihood that the benefit obligation will be paid.

The rationale for the actuaries approach is as follows: because funds are to be set aside to pay an obligation in the future, the amount that has to be set aside should consider the rate of the return on the investment. For example, given an expected return of 10%, a \$100 obligation payable in one year would be valued at \$90.91 in today's dollars (\$100 ÷ 1.1 = \$90.91), and \$90.91 could be set aside today to pay the \$100 future obligation.

The rationale for the approach favored by financial economists is that pension obligations should be discounted based on the likelihood that they will be received by plan participants. Because participants are very likely to receive most of their pension benefits (for example, because of vesting provisions in ERISA and PBGC guaranties), their pension benefits should be discounted using a discount rate close to the risk-free rate. Financial economists say that the actuaries' approach may make an inappropriate connection between the value of liabilities and the rate of return on assets. For example, the value of the obligation can be increased or decreased by changing the assumption on the rate of return, which suggests that a pension plan could eliminate some of its underfunding by investing the plan's assets in riskier investments.[49]

The approach suggested by some actuaries results in discount rates that are generally higher than the rates that result by using the approach suggested by some financial economists. One effect of this divergence of opinion is that the value of pension plan benefit obligations is higher (and funding ratios are lower) using the approach favored by some financial economists. For example, in March 2012, one study estimated the underfunding of multiemployer DB pension plans at $101 billion under the actuaries' approach and $428 billion under the financial economists' approach.[50]

End Notes

[1] See Bulletin 2776, National Compensation Survey: Employee Benefits in the United States, March 2013, available at http://www.bls.gov/ncs/ebs/benefits/2013/ebbl0052.pdf.

[2] In some defined contribution (DC) plans, plan participants have the option to purchase annuities (a monthly payment for life) with some or all of their account balances. In some defined benefit (DB) plans, plan participants have the option to receive a lump-sum payment at retirement in lieu of the annuity.

[3] The Government Accountability Office (GAO) indicated that about 0.7% of pension plans were multiple employer pension plans. See U.S. Government Accountability Office, Federal Agencies Should Collect Data and Coordinate Oversight of Multiple Employer Plans, GAO-12-665, September 13, 2012, p. 10, http://www.gao.gov/assets/650/ 648285.pdf.

[4] The Pension Benefit Guaranty Corporation (PBGC) was created in the Employee Retirement Income Security Act of 1974 (ERISA) to insure private-sector DB pension plans. For more information on PBGC, see CRS Report 95-118, Pension Benefit Guaranty Corporation (PBGC): A Primer, by John J. Topoleski

[5] Although participants' benefits will be paid in the future, the sponsors of qualified DB pension plans are generally required to make contributions to the plan each year for benefits earned in that year.

[6] See Department of Labor (DOL), Employee Benefits Security Administration, Department of Labor, Employee Benefits Security Administration, Private Pension Plan Bulletin Abstract of 2010 Form 5500 Annual Reports, November 2012.

[7] The annual maximum benefit is $57,477 for individuals who begin receiving their benefits at the age of 65 and whose plan is terminated in 2013. For more information on the termination of single employer DB pension plans, see CRS Report RS22624, The Pension Benefit Guaranty Corporation and Single-Employer Plan Terminations, by Jennifer A. Staman and Erika K. Lunder.

[8] See DOL, Employee Benefits Security Administration, Private Pension Plan Bulletin Historical Tables and Graphs: 1975-2011, June 2013, http://www.dol.gov/ebsa/pdf/ historicaltables. pdf.

[9] In single employer plans, participants receive a monthly payment in retirement that is based on a formula that typically uses a combination of length of service, accrual rate, and average of final years' salary. For example, a plan might specify that retirees receive an amount equal to 1.5% of their proscribed pay for each year of service, where the proscribed pay is the average of a worker's highest five pay years. A worker with 20 years of service in a DB plan that has accrual rate of 1.5% that is based on an average of the worker's highest five years of salary of $50,000 would receive a pension benefit of $50,000 x 20 x 0.015 = $15,000 per year.

[10] See National Compensation Survey: Employee Benefits in the United States, March 2011National Compensation Survey, March 2011, available at http://www.bls. gov/ncs/ ebs/benefits/2011/ebbl0048.pdf.

[11] The plans, apart from the TSP, are named for the section of the tax code that authorized them. Private-sector employers establish 401(k) plans, public school systems and nonprofits establish 403(b) plans, and state and local governments and nonprofits establish 457(b) plans.

[12] The funding rules for multiemployer DB pension plans are found at 26 U.S.C. §431.

[13] Investment losses and investment gains are also called experience losses and experiences gains, respectively.

[14] Pension plans are able to amortize experience gains and losses and changes in benefits as a result of changes to actuarial assumptions. Amortization means that plans can spread out the effect of these events over a specified number of years. For example, funding shortfalls as a result of investment losses are generally required to make up over a period of 15 years, although a provision in the Preservation of Access to Care for Medicare Beneficiaries and Pension Relief Act of 2010 (P.L. 111-192) allowed investment losses from 2008 or 2009 to be amortized over a period of 30 years. For more information on this amortization of experience gains and losses, see U.S. Congress, Joint Committee on Taxation, General Explanation Of Tax Legislation Enacted In The 111th Congress, committee print, 111th Cong., 2nd sess., March 2011, JCS-1-11 (Washington: GPO, 2011).

[15] See PBGC, Multiemployer Pension Plans: Report to Congress Required by the Pension Protection Act of 2006, January 22, 2013, p. 7, http://www.pbgc.gov/documents/pbgc-report-multiemployer-pension-plans.pdf.

[16] For more information, see Withdrawal Liability, PBGC, available at http://www.pbgc. gov/prac/multiemployer/ withdrawal-liability.html or Keith R. McMurdy, Esq., Multiemployer Withdrawal Liability: Understanding the Basics, Fox Rothschild LLP, http://www.google.com/url?sa=t&rct=j&q=&esrc=s&source=web&cd=1&cad=rja&ved= 0CCoQFjAA&url= http%3A%2F%2Fwww.foxrothschild.com%2FuploadedFiles% 2Fattorneys%2FdeskReference_mcmurdy_multiemployerWithdrawalLiability2.pdf&ei=YMI5Uu XlPKfD4AO91 YHABA&usg= AFQjCNGOQkMaGuR3KJYtlvSBSyCz_eGzNw&sig2 =0IZ41Pi 2bIgb2Zj_c2QioQ&bvm=bv.52288139,d.dmg.

[17] As of the date of this report, there is no proposal in the 113th Congress to deal with orphan participants. In the 111th Congress, Senator Bob Casey introduced S. 3157, the Create Jobs and Save Benefits Act of 2010, which, among other provisions, would have transferred the liabilities for orphan participants to PBGC. Plans would have been required to transfer to PBGC sufficient assets from which to pay for five years of benefit payments. For more information, see Senator Bob Casey, "Casey Pension Bill Would Protect Benefits and

Remove Burden on Companies Contributing to Multi-Employer Plans," press release, March 22, 2010, http://www.casey.senate.gov/newsroom/releases/casey-pensionbill-would-protect-benefits-and-remove-burden-on-companies-contributing-to-multi-employer-plans.

[18] Each pension plan has an actuary that makes estimates of a variety of factors that affect the plan, such as the number of current and future plan participants, current and future plan funding, and future contributions.

[19] The funding statuses are available at http://www.dol.gov/ebsa/criticalstatusnotices.html.

[20] Ibid.

[21] PBGC indicated that the total number of plan certifications is less than the total number of multiemployer DB pension plans because some plans are terminated but continue to pay benefits (wasting trusts) and are required to file annual Form 5500 reports but are not required to file zone certifications. See PBGC, Multiemployer Pension Plans: Report to Congress Required by the Pension Protection Act of 2006, January 22, 2013, p. 40, http://www.pbgc.gov/ documents/pbgc-report-multiemployer-pension-plans.pdf.

[22] See PBGC, FY2013 Annual Report, November 15, 2013, http://www.pbgc.gov/ res/reports/ ar2013.html.

[23] The remaining amount ($87 million) consisted of cash holdings, receivables, and net capitalized assets.

[24] The remaining amount ($46 million) consisted of payables and future benefits to trusteed plans.

[25] See PBGC, FY 2012 PBGC Exposure Report, http://www.pbgc.gov/documents/2012-exposure-report.pdf.

[26] This is reportedly the Central States Pension Fund. Among many references to this plan, see, for example, U.S. Congress, House Committee on Education and the Workforce, Subcommittee on Health, Employment, Labor, and Pensions, Examining the Challenges Facing PBGC and Defined Benefit Pension Plans, 112th Cong., 2nd sess., February 2, 2012, 112-50 (Washington: GPO, 2012) and Testimony of Thomas C. Nyhan, executive director and general counsel, Central States Southeast and Southwest Areas Pension Fund, in U.S. Congress, House Committee on Education and the Workforce, Subcommittee on Health, Employment, Labor, and Pensions, "Strengthening the Multiemployer Pension System: How Will Proposed Reforms Affect Employers, Workers and Retirees?," 113th Cong., 1st sess., October 29, 2013.

[27] This is reportedly the United Mineworkers of America 1974 Pension Plan. See U.S. Congress, House Committee on Natural Resources, The CARE Act, report to accompany H.R. 5479, 111th Cong., H.Rept. 111-651.

[28] This is calculated as follows: 12 x [($11 x 30) + (.75 x $33 x 30)]. For reference, the maximum benefit payable to participants in single employer DB pension plans that are trusteed by PBGC is higher than the multiemployer program maximum benefit. It depends on the year of plan termination, the age at which the participant begins to receive the benefit, and the form of the benefit. For example, the single employer maximum benefit is $57,500 for an individual who is in a plan that is terminated in 2013, begins to receive the benefit at the age of 65, and receives the benefit in the form of a single life annuity. The maximum benefit is $23,278 for an individual who is in a plan that is terminated in 2013, begins to receive the benefit at the age of 55, and receives a joint-and-survivor annuity.

[29] This is calculated as $1.9 billion from plans that had been terminated but had not yet started receiving assistance and $6.7 billion from plans that are ongoing but expected to become insolvent within 10 years.

[30] Testimony of Hon. Joshua Gotbaum, PBGC Director, in U.S. Congress, House Committee on Education and the Workforce, Subcommittee on Health, Employment, Labor and Pensions, March 5, 2013, http://edworkforce.house.gov/ uploadedfiles/gotbaum_testimony.pdf.

[31] For example, the Subcommittee on Health, Employment, Labor, and Pensions in the House Education and Workforce Committee has held six hearings since January 2012 on the subject of multiemployer DB pension plans.

[32] For example, Phil Roe, chairman of the Subcommittee on Health, Employment, Labor, and Pensions in the House Education and Workforce Committee said that "[m]aintaining the status quo is no longer possible. Provisions in the law governing multiemployer pensions will expire in two years, which means Congress has an important opportunity to study the system, assess its strengths and weaknesses, and pursue solutions that support workers without discouraging participation in the voluntary pension system." See U.S. Congress, House Committee on Education and the Workforce, Subcommittee on Health, Employment, Labor, and Pensions, Challenges Facing Multiemployer Pension Plans: Evaluating PBGC's Insurance Program and Financial Outlook, 112th Cong., 2nd sess., December 19, 2012.

[33] See GAO, Multiemployer Plans and PBGC Face Urgent Challenges, GAO-13-428T, March 5, 2013, http://www.gao.gov/assets/660/652687.pdf.

[34] An analysis of the amount by which premiums would rise is beyond the scope of this paper. PBGC's reasonably possible scenario shows an increase in the liability of PBGC of $36.7 billion (which would not be due in one year but would be spread out over the lifetimes of plan participants). There were approximately 10.6 million participants in multiemployer DB pensions in 2011. Each participant's share of the $27 billion liability would be approximately $2,600. For reference, in 2014, plan sponsors pay $12 per participant in PBGC multiemployer insurance premiums.

[35] See PBGC, FY2013 Projections Report, http://www.pbgc.gov/documents/Projections-report-2013.pdf.

[36] The estimate of new claims was much larger than the estimate of financial assistance because net claims include benefits that will paid after FY2024, but the value of financial assistance includes only assistance provided within the next 10 years.

[37] The website of the NCCMP is http://www.nccmp.org.

[38] The proposal, Solutions Not Bailouts, is available at http://www.solutionsnotbailouts.com

[39] As of the date of this report, the Congressional Research Service (CRS) is aware of only NCCMP's proposal for multiemployer DB pension reform.

[40] See ERISA 4002 §1302(g)(2) and 29 U.S.C. 1302 §(g)(2).

[41] For example, Chairman Phil Roe and Ranking Member Robert Andrews of the Subcommittee on Health, Employment, Labor, and Pensions in the House Education and Workforce Committee have both expressed reservations about providing government financial assistance for PBGC. See U.S. Congress, House Committee on Education and the Workforce, Subcommittee on Health, Employment, Labor, and Pensions, Examining the Challenges Facing PBGC and Defined Benefit Pension Plans, 112th Cong., 2nd sess., February 2, 2012, 112-50 (Washington: GPO, 2012) and U.S. Congress, House Committee on Education and the Workforce, Subcommittee on Health, Employment, Labor, and Pensions, Strengthening the Multiemployer Pension System: What Reforms Should Policymakers Consider?, 113th Cong., 1st sess., June 12, 2013.

[42] See, for example, the following: testimony of Teresa Ghilarducci before the U.S. Congress, House Education and Workforce, Subcommittee on Health, Employment, Labor, and Pensions, Strengthening the Multiemployer Pension System: What Reforms Should Policymakers Consider?, 113th Cong., 1st sess., June 12, 2013; statement by the Pension

Rights Center, "Statement of the Pension Rights Center the Subcommittee on Health, Education, Labor and Pensions Committee on Education and Workforce U.S. House of Representatives For [sic] a hearing on 'Strengthening the Multiemployer Pension System: What Reforms Should Policymakers Consider?'," press release, June 12, 2013, http://www.pensionrights.org/publications/fact-sheet/benefit-cutbacks-multiemployer-plans; statement by the National Electrical Contractors Association, "Statement of the National Electrical Contractors Association to the Subcommittee on Health, Education, Labor and Pensions Committee on Education and Workforce U.S. House of Representatives For [sic] a hearing on "Strengthening the Multiemployer Pension System: What Reforms Should Policymakers Consider?"," press release, June 12, 2013, http://www.necanet. org/docs/ default-source/attachments/20130612_necastatement-pension-hearing.pdf?sfvrsn=2; and the testimony of David Certner, legislative policy director for the American Association of Retired Persons (AARP), before the U.S. Congress, House Education and Workforce, Subcommittee on Health, Employment, Labor, and Pensions, "Strengthening the Multiemployer Pension System: How Will Proposed Reforms Affect Employers, Workers, and Retirees?" 113th Cong., 1st sess., October 29, 2013.

[43] For example, typically a multiemployer pension plan's board of trustees has equal representation from labor and management, which may or may not adequately represent retirees' concerns.

[44] DB pension plan assets are generally invested in stocks and bonds and might include other assets such as private equity and real estate. Pension plan assets that are invested in a conservative manner would likely hold more bonds and less stock and other assets than pension plans invested in a more aggressive manner.

[45] See 26 U.S.C. §431.

[46] See, for example, monetary policy statements issued by the Federal Open Market Committee, available at http://www.federalreserve.gov/monetarypolicy/fomccalendars.htm.

[47] The discount rate used by multiemployer DB pension plans to value plan liabilities is generally the expected rate of return on plan assets, whereas the discount rate used by single employer DB pension plans is an average of corporate bond interest rates. For more information, see CRS Report 95-118, Pension Benefit Guaranty Corporation (PBGC): A Primer, by John J. Topoleski

[48] The context for much of the recent policy discussions on the appropriate rate for discounting pensions has been in the area of pension plans for state and local government employees. Although there are many differences between state and local government pension plans and multiemployer DB pension plans (for example, state and local government plans are much less likely to become insolvent), many aspects of the discount rate discussion apply to all DB pension plans, including multiemployer plans. For more information, see Milliman, Setting the Discount Rate for Pension Liabilities, July 2012, http://publications.milliman. com/periodicals/peri/ pdfs/PERi-07-17-2012.pdf; Douglas Elliot, State and Local Pension Funding Deficits: A Primer, Brookings Institution, December 2010, http://www. brookings.edu/~/media/research/files/reports/2010/12/06%20state%20local%20funding%20 elliott/1206_state_local_funding_elliott.pdf; The American Academy of Actuaries and the Society of Actuaries, Pension Actuary's Guide to Financial Economics, 2006, http://www.soa.org/Files/Sections/actuary-journal-final.pdf; and Congressional Budget Office, The Underfunding of State and Local Pension Plans, May 2011, http://www. cbo.gov/sites/default/files/cbofiles/ftpdocs/120xx/doc12084/05- 04-pensions.pdf.

[49] However, CRS is not aware of any reports of pension plans using this hypothetical strategy to lower the plan's underfunding.

[50] See David Zion, Amit Varshney, and Nichole Burnap, Crawling Out of the Shadows: Shining a Light on Multiemployer Pension Plans, Credit Suisse - Equity Research, March 25, 2012, https://doc.research-andanalytics.csfb.com/docView?language=ENG&source=ulg&format=PDF&document_id=957405261&serialid=e7HNjCiguHeLKc%2FL2JnKohP%2FMTt9zyVVnhUWwxM%2FGlk%3D.

INDEX

D

E

F

N

O

P

R

S

T

U

V

W

Y